Catch the New Wind

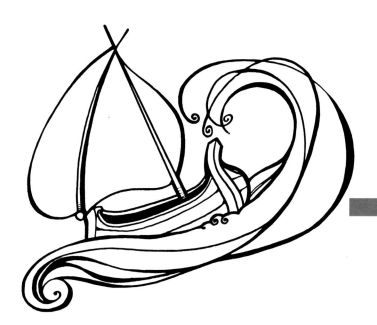

Word Books, Publisher
Waco, Texas

Catch the New Wind

Marilee Zdenek and Marge Champion

To

Al Tamara
Gina

Gower Blake
Gregg

whose roots
go deep in
love

Thank you Lord, for:

Jean and Jack Pegram

Steve Allen

Keith Clark

Bill Norris

Shirley and Grover Brown

Lou and Coke Evans

Jim Collier

John West

Rabbi Allen Secher

Ross Greek

Father Clarence Rivers

Donn Moomaw

and for all those who felt the New Wind and helped us hoist the sail.

Gary Demarest

Perla Earle

Corita Kent

Jack Durkee

CONTENTS

This book does not put down
traditional services
organ music
black clerical robes
19th century hymns
ladies with hats
or men with ties.....

However....

8

If you're ready to have some new experiences in worship, we would like to provide a framework through which your own creativity may flow...

to be spontaneous
to be free
to be improvisational
to allow for moment-to-moment
happenings
to make room for the movement
of the Holy Spirit

You are encouraged to draw from
the best of our " happenings "

leave out our mistakes,
surpass all of our efforts,

And inspire others to begin —

Marilee Zdenek
Marge Champion

may the Holy Spirit ZAP you until you tingle with joy!

"They who wait for the Lord shall renew their strength, they shall Mount Up With Wings Like Eagles, they shall run and not be weary, they shall walk and not faint."

(Isaiah 40:31)

13

If you're ready to fly
there's always someone
who wants to stand
on
your
wings....

remember: love is patient and kind,
even to confirmed traditionalists!

14

I. Straight from the Source

"Make a joyful noise unto the Lord" (Psalm 98:4)
with electronic sound
and rock and folk and all "now" music
recorded music and live music

Renaissance instruments
primitive African instruments
homemade earthy instruments
delicate Baroque instruments
maracas
and yes, very much yes, a flute

"Praise Him with loud clashing cymbals"

(Psalm 150:5)

DID YOU KNOW THAT JOHN CALVIN WENT ALL OVER SWITZERLAND DESTROYING ORGANS BECAUSE HE DIDN'T THINK THEY BELONGED IN CHURCHES?

What makes one instrument sacred and another instrument secular?

Is an organ really more holy than a guitar?

"Sing to the Lord a New Song"

(Psalm 96:1)

My Sweet Lord...
He Ain't Heavy, He's My Brother....
You've Got a Friend...
We'll Walk Hand in Hand...
Tell It All, Brother....

18

(But don't forget the old songs...)

Amazing Grace...
The Spirit Is a-Movin'...
Go Tell It on the Mountain....
Let Us Break Bread Together...
Morning Has Broken

"And King David danced before the Lord with all his might" (II Samuel 6:14)

let's use:

liturgical dancers
our own children as dancers
local college dancers
professional or ethnic dancers

Quietly and reverently
to "The Lord's Prayer"
Wildly and ecstatically
to "Oh Happy Day"

on the altar
up and down the aisles

20

" *Let them praise His name with dancing* "

(Psalm 149:3)

Involve the congregation in movement —

Swaying,
Turning,
Arms uplifted,
Reaching to God,

around each other

"God does not live in houses built by men"

(Acts 7:48)

So....Create a Celebration...

In the parking lot
and dance the hora
(get a Jewish friend
    to lead it)

On the beach and fly kites
In the hills or prairies
(bring raisin cake
    and wild honey)

HAVE
COMMUNION
AT DAWN ON
THE DESERT

find a lake and name it Galilee

"Praise the Lord, you flying birds"

(Psalm 148:7-10)

"Beautify the House of the Lord"

(Ezra 7:27)

Decorate the sanctuary

with banners of many colors
with huge paper hangings
with balloon trees~

Stained glass windows are elegant and beautiful but are they really more worshipful than these creative love-gifts from the people?

"Greetings to all God's people "
(James 1:1)

Let's use bright paper joy programs
for everyone to keep (Remember when they were
black and white and called the
Sunday bulletin?)

Now: strong color, fit to frame,
local artists, silk screen,
children's crayola drawings,

covered with poems,
inspirationals, words to the songs,
prayers, serendipities,
and promises....

And Jesus touched him and he was healed.
And Jesus **TOUCHED** him and he was healed.
And Jesus **TOUCHED** him and he was healed.
And Jesus **TOUCHED** him and he was healed.

(Luke 5:13)

Would you like to reach out
and touch the hand of the
person next to you? ....

and pray for him?

touch................touch..................touch

"And they were filled with
the Holy Spirit"

(Acts 2:4)

I have been touched by joy —
the world is beautiful!

27

"Hear my prayer, O Lord"

(Psalm 143:1)

the people sing: God the Father, hear our prayer.
Hear us, God the Son.
Holy Spirit, hear our prayer.
Mercy on Your People, Lord.

then silence until
someone feels led to pray ....
and the people respond with: God the Father, hear our prayer.
Hear us, God the Son.
Holy Spirit, hear our prayer.
Mercy on Your People, Lord.

again silence ...
until someone else
offers a prayer, then the people sing the response

Silence .... Prayer .... Response
Silence .... Prayer .... Response

and the leader closes with a prayer... and amen.

"Thy Word is a lamp unto my feet, and a light unto my path"

(Psalm 119: 105)

let the people
read the Scripture —

..... from different places in the room
..... children, old people and teenagers

..... short Scripture selections (readers who speak out)
..... mixed with secular readings that support the theme —
— poetry
— one-minute stories

"All thy works shall give thanks to Thee, O Lord"

(Psalm 145:10)

Praise
Him
with :

film, and slides, drama and improvisations, the list is as endless as the creativity of man —

30

"*How shall we sing the Lord's song in a foreign land?*"

(Psalm 137:4)

"SEE THE MAN WHO CAN SAVE YOU THE MOST"

"PUT A TIGER IN YOUR TANK"

"FLY UNITED"

"THE BIG 'G' STANDS FOR GOODNESS"

"COME ALIVE"

"MAKE THE MOST OF THEIR WONDER YEARS"

Thank you, Sister Mary Corita, for teaching us that even Madison Avenue can sing His praises.

"COME TO WHERE THE FLAVOR IS"

"THE BEST TO YOU EACH MORNING"

31

"I was a stranger and you welcomed me"

(Matthew 25:35)

Let's talk more in church
to strangers
(and friends)

Before the service,
at structured times
during the service,

casually,
in encounter,
in conversational prayer,
in dialogue —

"Man looks on the outward appearance but the Lord looks on the heart " (I Samuel 16:7)

Invite them to come from the drag strips or the hills—
bearded and long-haired
and hungry for God.

Remember—many have never been inside a church before
but they will come—
rebellious, lonely, joyful, seeking.

Let them hear their music
blasting from the sanctuary
and dare to believe that
God is not turned off by jeans.

"Take no thought for what ye shall put on"

(Matthew 6:25)

Wouldn't you love to be in a church where bare foot, blue-jeaned children could sit on the floor and really be comfortable in their Father's house?

If we dress up so much on the outside, don't we tend to dress up the inside too, and bring to God a "presentable self" instead of the real one?

34

"Let the children come to me"

(Mark 10:14)

Let's make it
easy for them
to come.

35

So,
    let's praise Him
    with shouts of joy
      and whispers of longings
    and adore Him
    with an
      effervescent faith —
    for

The Lord does not delight
    in our solemnity.

Where the Spirit of the Lord is, There is Freedom!

II. Walking through Seven Celebrations

Invite the community— weeks ahead

For each service, use colorful joy programs covered with
the words to the songs, prayers and readings. The art
work for ours was done by teenagers and is shown
on the first two pages of each service.

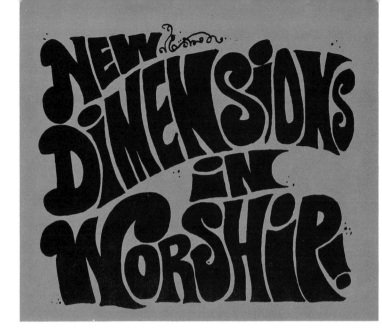

NEW DIMENSIONS IN WORSHIP

BEL AIR PRESBYTERIAN CHURCH

16221 Mulholland Drive

October 4
Let There Be Joy

October 11
Treasure Hunt – The Serendipities of God

October 18
Walls Come Tumbling Down

October 25
The Good Earth

November 1
The Risk of Caring

November 8
Man For All Seasons

November 15
Expressions of Love – Candlelight Communion

6:00 P.M.

sharp!

Let There Be Joy

As the people enter, children give them programs

SWEET SONG OF SALVATION

Tony:
When you know a pretty story
You don't let it go unsaid,
You tell it to your children
As you tuck them into bed.
And when you know a wonderful secret
You tell it to your friends,
Because a lifetime filled with happiness
Is like a street that never ends.

Tony:
Look around you as you sing it
There are people everywhere,
And to those who stop to listen
This sweet song becomes a prayer.
Cause when you know a wonderful secret
You tell it to your friends,
Tell them that a lifetime filled with Jesus
Is like a street that never ends.

Everybody:
Sing that sweet, sweet song of salvation
And let your laughter fill the air,
Sing that sweet, sweet song of salvation
And tell the people everywhere,
Sing that sweet, sweet song of salvation
To every man, every nation
Sing that sweet, sweet song of salvation
And let the people know that Jesus cares.

Everybody:
Sing that sweet, sweet song of salvation
And let your laughter fill the air,
Sing that sweet, sweet song of salvation
And tell the people everywhere,
Sing that sweet, sweet song of salvation
To every man, every nation
Sing that sweet, sweet song of salvation
And let the people know that Jesus cares.

comeonpeoplenowweneedmorehelp! weneedsingersanddancersandmusicmakers!

NEW DIMENSIONS IN WORSHIP

Director of Creative Worship	Marilee Zdenek
Creative Advisors	Marge Champion Jim Collier
Production Manager	Jack Durkee
Light and Sound	Jack Pegram Bruce Bidlack
Music	Keith Clark Linda Gyman Tony Harris Fred Bock
Art	Jean Pegram Ladd O'Dell Ron Riddick Simone Grant Tony Penido Marty Reitsen
Dance	John West
High School and College Coordinator	Jim Smoke
Publicity	Michelle Gregory
Secretarial	Betty Travis
Road Runners	Carol Richardson Liz Gonia

Bel Air
Presbyterian Church

weneedphotographersandprintersandroadrunnersandsilkscreeners:· yes!yes!

weneedwritersandpaintersandactorsandballoonblowerupers. weneedyou!yes

whattheworldneedsnowismorecreativepeopleonthiscommittee! weneedyou! ·-

45

Rehavia Yakovee and Avremi Manzur are performing an ancient Hebrew dance of praise, as it might have been done by any of the religious leaders at that time. Our Israeli guests show us how it was really done, before we stopped showing emotion, and before we forgot that God knows how to smile.

Can you believe, actually BELIEVE that King David danced up and down the streets when he brought the ark of the Lord into Jerusalem?

Can you imagine the Old Testament prophets playing the drums, trumpets and tambourines and shouting praises to God in a Worship Service?

The congregation participates in an Israeli dance (the hora) to the music "Hava Nageela" ("Come Let Us Rejoice and Sing"). The benediction is offered after the dance. The people have participated in the worship service as they offer this physical expression of their praise.

What if God danced instead of walked?
What if there were no pipe organs in
heaven and the angels played
guitars, triangles and tambourines?
What if cherubs told jokes and Saint Peter
laughed a lot?
What if finger painting were required
and heavenly board meetings were
held on a merry-go-round where
everyone could interrupt?

What else could Easter mean?
What else could all that running
from tomb to city with post-
funeral picnics by the sea mean,
except that God's a holiday in my head
and life with Him a party?

Herbert B. Barks, Jr.

LET THERE BE JOY

THEME: This is a service of praise and adoration. Enthusiasm can be as worshipful as solemnity. Let's praise Him in joy—with song, with dance, with fellowship.

SECTION AND RESPONSIBILITY	SCRIPT	ADDENDA
1. Art	Set design: banners, professional posters, and homemade hangings.	Use dozens of posters; get teenagers involved in making them—even the little kids. Locate material at art festivals, book or stationery stores, or write poster companies listed on p. 187.
2. Sound Music research	Pre-service music starts (on tape)† 1. "I'm On My Way" (Mahalia Jackson) 2. "I Just Want to Celebrate" (Rare Earth) 3. "What the World Needs Now" (Burt Bacharach) 4. "Oh, Happy Day!" (Edwin Hawkins Singers) 5. "Sweet Sweet Song of Salvation" (Larry Norman)	Feel free to change the songs, depending upon popularity and availability. We suggest you transfer 15 minutes of records to tape for continuity. We liked a balance of folk, rock, gospel, and popular. Locate material in record stores, teenage collections.
Film	Projections on a 12-foot screen are changing throughout the service (joyful photographs and pictures transferred to slides).	
3. Minister	A warm welcome with a conversational quality	
4. Music man	He leads the congregation in two songs backed up by guitars, kids, choir, etc. 1. "The Joy Song" (p. 183) 2. "Sweet Sweet Song of Salvation" (p. 184; lyrics, p. 44). For soloist and congregation.	The music man must be casual and able to help the people relax. If the congregation does not know "The Joy Song," you may want to substitute something they are familiar with for the opening selection.††

GOOFS WE MADE: †Our tendency was to "blast them out" . . . we lost some from sheer volume.
††"Sweet Sweet Song of Salvation" was too hard for our congregation to sing. Wish we had used this as a solo or chosen something like "Oh, Happy Day."

54

SECTION AND RESPONSIBILITY	SCRIPT	ADDENDA
5. Drama	Spiritual graffiti (Scripture, secular readings, prayer)	Choose five readers of varying ages and sex.
	1. "The Kingdom of Heaven" (pp. 57, 186)	
Film	2. Film: "Psalm for a Surfer" (p. 187)	
	3. Psalm 150, selections (p. 57)	
	4. Luke 1, selections (p. 58)	
	5. "It's a Groovy Day, Lord" (pp. 58, 186)	
6. Music man	Choir: "Oh, Sing to the Lord a New Song" (p. 183)	Old Testament anthem with tambourines and finger cymbals
7. Minister†	Develop this basic theme: God created us with a need to express our emotions. The Psalms are a good reminder that God does not delight in our solemnity, for He created laughter and called us to praise His name with dancing.	He could incorporate the reading by Herbert Barks, p. 53.
8. Film	One-minute film: "Creatures, Bless the Lord" (p. 187)	A contemporary psalm
9. Minister	Invites the offering and the people sing "Rock-a-My-Soul" (p. 184) while children with straw baskets collect the gifts.	
10. Music	Choir: "Hava Nageela" (p. 182)	The extra effort to sing this in Hebrew was really meaningful.
11. Minister	He introduces the guest rabbi. The rabbi talks about dance as a form of worship and introduces a Yemenite dance as it might have been done at the time of David. Then he tells the meaning and significance of "Hava Nageela" ("Come Let Us Rejoice and Sing").	Invite a local rabbi who is interested in creative and ecumenical services. Invite his friends! Ask him to read "It's a Groovy Day, Lord" (sec. 5).

GOOFS WE MADE: †We forgot to check our minister's wardrobe; ties and jackets just don't make it! Sport shirts or sweaters on the clergy help people to relax—especially young people.

SECTION AND RESPONSIBILITY	SCRIPT	ADDENDA
Film	Film: *His Land*. Use excerpt from this film, showing the hora being danced.	Film strips are not available; however, you can rent the entire film *His Land* (p. 187) and show the complete movie on another occasion. If you don't want to do that, you could substitute a live demonstration by asking the rabbi to recommend a few people to dance the hora in church.
12. Music	The accordionist picks up the last note of the film and everyone follows him out to the parking lot to dance the hora.	You'll need an accordionist for the congregational dance, and a good sound system outside.
13. Minister	He offers the benediction after the dance, restating that the dance was our praise to God, expressed in our total involvement—a physical expression of our faith—our celebration to the glory of God.	Parking lot may be lighted by the headlights from the cars. Be sure to have volunteers there early to park cars, designating a large space to be used for the dance.

Shalom

The Kingdom of Heaven Is Like an Open Hydrant on a Hot Summer
   Day

—a geyser of water in the air, spraying water high above the street
—a brilliant white shower against the dark tenements, cooling their
   sunbaked bricks
—a gushing river in the gutter liberating the imagination of children
—the Kingdom of Heaven is like a living stream where life meets life

                                                        Kevin McNiff

Psalm 150

Praise the Lord! . . . . with trumpet sound
      praise him with lute and harp!
Praise him with timbrel and dance
      praise him with strings and pipe!
Praise him with sounding cymbals;
      praise him with loud clashing cymbals!
Let everything that breathes praise the Lord!
      Praise the Lord!

                              —Revised Standard Version

Selections
from Luke I

My heart is overflowing with praise of my Lord;
    my soul is full of joy in God, my Savior.
He has set kings down from their thrones
    and lifted up the humble.
He has satisfied the hungry with good things
    and sent the rich away with empty hands.
Yes, he has helped Israel, his child;
He has remembered the mercy that he promised to our
    forefathers, to Abraham and his sons for evermore!

                    —J. B. Phillips' translation

Prayer: "It's a Groovy Day, Lord"

It was like a groovy day, Lord: warm, bright and
no smog. So I took a walk. Only down the street,
but a bird sang and some guy was cutting his lawn.
And this little kid was eating ice cream, and it
was like WOW! Caught the whiff of a flower—
lovely. It was a turned on day, Lord, and I walked
into town and the world seemed with it. I saw
people and I felt people and I heard people, and I
wanted to stretch out my hands and shout: "I love
you, I love you!"—but I didn't, and neither did
they, but it was a groovy day, Lord.

                    —Rabbi Allen Secher

Treasure Hunt—
The Serendipities of God

316 West Manhattan Avenue
Santa Fe, New Mexico 87501
988-8080

Treasure Hunt

The Serendipities of GOD

THE WEDDING BANQUET

Chorus: I cannot come, I cannot come to the banquet,
don't trouble me now
I have married a wife, I have bought me a cow.
I have fields and commitments that cost a pretty sum.
Pray, hold me excused, I cannot come.

① A certain man held a feast on his fine estate in town.
He laid a festive table and wore a wedding gown.
He sent invitations to his neighbors far and wide.
But when the meal was ready, each of them replied:

② The master rose up in anger, called his servants by name,
Said, "Go into the town, fetch the blind and the lame.
Fetch the peasant and the pauper, for this I have willed,
My banquet must be crowded and my table must be filled!"

③ Now God has written a lesson for the rest of mankind.
If we're slow in responding, he may leave us behind.
He's preparing a table for that great and glorious day.
When the Lord and Master calls us, be certain not to say:

When Jesus taught, he often spoke in parables. When he spoke with farmers, he talked about crops; when he talked with shepherds, he spoke of sheep. Today he might speak to us about the parable of the skyscrapers, the freeways, or even balloons.

Did you ever try to play catch with a balloon? It doesn't work. We can't control where the balloon goes, or who receives it, or the wind that carries it.

The Parable of the Balloon

Everyone was happy at the birthday party except one little boy. He had all the usual problems that shy little guys have. He wanted to have fun just like everybody else, but something inside him just always got all tied up. He could never really bring himself to reach out to others, so even the times that should have been the happiest were lonely times for him. He wanted to reach out and be a part of things but he just didn't know how.

One of the other boys picked up a balloon and tapped it to one of his friends. But balloons don't always go where they are tapped. The wind took the balloon on its way until it touched the shoulder of the shy, frightened guy. He didn't know that the balloon wasn't meant for him, and for the first time in his life he felt like he was part of the party, and he really thought that someone had tapped the balloon to him. He took the balloon and with great excitement, he tapped it back. Soon he was playing with the others. A balloon that wasn't really meant for him somehow meant so very much to him.

God's blessings are like that, and we have the power to bring God's blessings to others. Sometimes the blessing we tap to a friend never gets there, and he never knows we sent it, and yet by the wind of the Spirit, God may send our blessings to someone we didn't even know was there.

63

The people listen to "The Parable of the Balloon" and then act out the meaning. As they tap the balloons to one another they say a blessing—"God loves you," "Have a joyful day," "God goes with you." They see the wind take the balloon in directions they never intended, just as God takes our blessings to others on the wind of the Spirit.

Herbert B. Banks, Jr.

If God doesn't fizz,
how come I feel all these bubbles?

TREASURE HUNT

THEME: A serendipity is an unexpected treasure discovered while seeking something else. As we seek first the kingdom of God, how delightful we find His serendipities!

SECTION AND RESPONSIBILITY	SCRIPT	ADDENDA
1. Art	Set design: banners, posters, and balloon trees. (See p. 187 for addresses of poster companies.)	If you are doing this for a large group, have the balloons stamped "Smile, God Loves You," or some other blessing, such as "Be Touched by His Love."
2. Film	Pre-service music with appropriate slides changing on the screen. 1. "Up, Up and Away" (Fifth Dimension) 2. "Who Am I?" (Petula Clark) 3. "Turn, Turn, Turn" (The Byrds) 4. "He Bought the Whole Field" (The Medical Mission Sisters) 5. "Flowers Never Bend with the Rainfall" (Paul Simon)	
3. Minister	He welcomes the people and prepares them to be open to the serendipities of God.	
4. Music man	He leads the congregation in two songs: 1. "Seek and Ye Shall Find" (p. 183) 2. "The Wedding Banquet" (p. 184; lyrics, p. 61). For soloist and congregation.	
5. Film	Slides: "Happiness Is"	These could be homemade slides; use your own imagination. How about pictures of your Sunday school kids and what they think happiness is? Tape their voices and match to the pictures.

SECTION AND RESPONSIBILITY	SCRIPT	ADDENDA
6. Minister	He tells the parable of the balloon† (text on p. 63), illustrating that balloons are like blessings—we can't control where they go. We can send them out but they may reach someone we never had in mind at all. Several teenagers take the balloons into the people and tap them to the people with a blessing.	We used a layman.
7. Film Drama	Spiritual graffiti 1. *The Giving Tree* (p. 186), slides with narrator 2. Parable of the house built on sand, Luke 6: 47-49 (p. 71) 3. Parable of the rich fool, Luke 12:16-21 (p. 71)	The child's book *The Giving Tree* is an exquisite story of unselfish love. Illustrate it with your own slides and choose one of your best readers to tell the story. You'll need two more readers for selections 2 and 3.
8. Minister Music man	He invites the offering as the music man leads the congregation in singing "Where Do I See God?" (p. 184)	
9. Minister	He leads the congregation in a short prayer, followed by silent prayer. The silence is broken by the record "Tell It All, Brother" (Kenny Rogers and The First Edition), a contemporary call to confession. With bowed heads, the people listen to the record and then wait in silence for a moment of meditation. This is followed by the record "Who Will Answer?" (Ed Ames), illustrated by slides.††	Make your own slides to illustrate the words.

GOOFS WE MADE: †We placed this much too early in the service. It should have followed section 12. Also, we should have taken longer with the parable so that the people would really be comfortable with the concept before we demonstrated that the balloons represented our blessings. Having learned our lesson, we used it again at the Celebration of Evangelism (Cincinnati, 1971). The fantastic impact there was truly a blessing

††We forgot to "Amen" the prayer, and half the people had their eyes closed through the slides!

SECTION AND RESPONSIBILITY	SCRIPT	ADDENDA
10. Drama	Spiritual graffiti 1. Matthew 13:44 (p. 72) 2. Matthew 13:45 (p. 72) 3. Matthew 6:33 (p. 72)	Choose three readers.
11. Minister	He introduces two people from the congregation, who share their blessings. Then he invites the congregation to share their concept of what it means to be a Christian. He brings this to a close when he feels the time is right.	Select a teenager and an older person (prechosen—don't just spring it on them).
12. Music man	He starts the singing again with 1. "Thank You, Jesus" (an original song by one of our teenagers; Sacred Songs has published one by the same title) 2. "Shalom" (p. 184)	

Luke 6:47–49

Everyone who comes to me, and listens to my words,
and obeys them—I will show you what he is like.
He is like a man who built a house: he dug deep
and laid the foundation on the rock. The river
flooded over and hit that house but it could not
shake it, because the house had been well built.
But the man who hears my words and does not obey
them is like a man who built a house on the ground
without laying a foundation; when the flood hit
that house it fell at once—what a terrible crash
that was!

Luke 12:16–21

Then Jesus told them this parable: ''A rich man
had land which bore good crops. He began to
think to himself, 'I don't have a place to keep
all my crops. What can I do? This is what I
will do,' he told himself; 'I will tear my barns
down and build bigger ones, where I will store
the grain and all my other goods. Then I will
say to myself; Lucky man! You have all the
good things you need for many years. Take life
easy, eat, drink, and enjoy yourself! But God
said to him, 'You fool! This very night you will
have to give up your life; then who will get all
these things you have kept for yourself?' '' And
Jesus concluded, ''This is how it is with those
who pile up riches for themselves but are not rich
from God's point of view.''

—Good News For Modern Man

Matthew 13:44

The kingdom of Heaven is like some treasure which
has been buried in a field. A man finds it and
buries it again, and goes off overjoyed to sell
all his possessions to buy himself that field.

Matthew 13:45

Or again, the kingdom of Heaven is like a
merchant searching for fine pearls. When he has
found a single pearl of great value, he goes and
sells all his possessions and buys it.

Matthew 6:33

So don't worry and don't keep saying, "What
shall we eat, what shall we drink or what shall
we wear?" That is what pagans are always looking
for; your Heavenly Father knows that you need them
all. Set your heart on his kingdom and his goodness,
and all these things will come to you as a
matter of course.

—J. B. Phillips' translation

Walls come Tumbling Down

WALLS

COME

TUMBLING

DOWN ...

JOSHUA FIT DE BATTLE OF JERICHO

Chorus:
Joshua fit de battle of-a Jericho,
Jericho, Jericho-o-o,
Joshua fit de battle of Jericho,
And de walls come-a-tumblin' down.

You may talk about your men of Gideon,
You may talk about your men of Saul;
But there's none like good old Joshua,
At de battle of Jericho,
That mornin' . . . . . .

Right up to the walls of Jericho,
He marched with spear in hand;
Old Joshua commanded the children to shout,
Cause de battle am in my hand,
That mornin' . . . . . .

PRAYER RESPONSE

God the Father, hear our prayer.
Hear us, God the Son.
Holy Spirit, hear our prayer.
Mercy on your people, Lord.

WALLS COME TUMBLING DOWN

THEME: We consider the walls that have developed between ourselves and others. Let's open our hearts to the Christian responsibility toward reconciliation.

SECTION AND RESPONSIBILITY	SCRIPT	ADDENDA
1. Art	Set design: posters and banners. "People are lonely because they build walls instead of bridges" etc.	Remember to change the theme of the posters—show division as well as redemption.
2. Sound	Pre-service music: 1. "I Am a Rock" (Paul Simon) 2. "Peace, My Friends" (Ray Repp) 3. "Sounds of Silence" (Simon and Garfunkel) 4. Disadvantages of Life (Silhouette Segments, Lutheran Church) 5. "Get Together" (Young Bloods) Locate material in record shops and teenage collections.	No slides this time because of so much film in this service. Disadvantages of Life is a spoken selection.†
3. Music man Minister Music man	Singers, kids with guitars, flute, tambourines, etc. 1. "Joshua Fit De Battle of Jericho" (p. 183; lyrics, p. 75) 2. Welcome 3. "They'll Know We Are Christians by Our Love" (p. 184)	When the welcome slips in between two songs, it adds a smooth continuity. (Don't sit down, music man!)
4. Minister or layman	Are we **really** one in the Spirit? Or do we sometimes build walls between ourselves and others? . . . etc.	Help them to be introspective. This could run four or five minutes.
5. Drama	Prayer: "I know it sounds corny, Jesus, but I'm lonely" by Malcolm Boyd (pp. 83, 186)	Earthy voice, male.

GOOFS WE MADE: †The spoken word (4) was not effective in pre-service. It might have worked better later in the program.

SECTION AND RESPONSIBILITY	SCRIPT	ADDENDA
6. Film	One-minute film: "Listen, Lady" (p. 187)—husband and wife: hostile	If possible, use two projectors—it helps the pacing. Otherwise splice the films together.†
7. Film	One-minute film: "The Kiss" (p. 187)—husband and wife: loving	
8. Music	Singer talks about the theme: The husband and wife reach out to each other and the walls come tumbling down. He sings: "The husband and the wife reach out to each other, and the walls come tumbling down."	Improvise melody loosely based on "Joshua Fit De Battle of Jericho"
9. Lay speaker	(Same speaker as section 4) And how about you parents and you teenagers—how about those walls?	
10. Drama Film	Dramatic improvisation—parent and teenager: hostile One-minute film: "Say 'Yes' to Love" (p. 187)—parent and child: redemptive	This will need some rehearsal, but avoid an exact script. Keep it improvisatory. Possible theme: (1) attending church (2) length of hair (3) choice of friends (4) any day-to-day hassle
11. Music	Singer from section 8 improvises: "And the parent and the child reach out to each other, and the walls come tumbling down."	It's important to use the same singer in sections 8, 11, and 14 to sustain continuity.
12. Film	One-minute film: "Person to Person" (p. 187)—race relations: hostile	
13. Dance	Dance: Blacks and whites dance to music from *West Side Story*—aggressive and hostile. But in the end they tear down the wall that is be-	Because of the type of music and dramatic emphasis of the choreography, more experienced dancers are required than for most

GOOFS WE MADE: †We didn't have two projectors and it made a big hole.

79

SECTION AND RESPONSIBILITY	SCRIPT	ADDENDA
	tween them and reach out to each other—race relations: redemptive† Note: Use three music themes— 1. "The Plum Is Too Ripe" *(Fantasticks)* 2. "Dance at the Gym" *(West Side Story)* 3. "There's a Place for Us" *(West Side Story)*	liturgical dance. Unless your talent is in this category, better import some people. The serendipity of this may well be that the next week the dancers come back as worshipers! (Creative evangelism?) To find skilled dancers, get help from an advanced modern dance group at a school or college or use trained professionals.
14. Music	Singer from sections 8 and 11: Improvises "The blacks and the whites reach out to each other, and the walls come tumbling down"; then, "All God's children reach out to each other, and the walls come tumbling down."	
15. Layman	Speaker from section 4: Expressions on the theme: What are the walls that separate us from each other? Do we know how to listen to each other? What difference does Christ make in all of this? Ask the people to find out the name of the person sitting next to them on both sides. (This will be important later.) Prayer: Direct them in silence before God to think of a wall that exists between someone and themselves . . . here in this room . . . at home . . . at the office . . . at school. Think about that wall. . . . Is there a way you could take the wall down? Could you go to that person and share your feelings? Doesn't Christ say, "Go and be reconciled to your brother"? Let's consider how we can tear down the walls.	

GOOFS WE MADE: †For some of our people this was too dramatic. We thought it was great. You choose.

SECTION AND RESPONSIBILITY	SCRIPT	ADDENDA
16. Drama Music man	I Corinthians 13, excerpt (p. 84). After inviting the offering, he sings: "Let's Get Together" (p. 183)†	Some rock instruments are really helpful.
17. Drama	Prayer: "I've searched for community in many places, Jesus" by Malcolm Boyd (pp. 83, 186)	Choose one reader.
18. Film Music Sound	Slides with music, "Bridge over Troubled Water" (Simon and Garfunkel)	Make your own slides to fit the words to "Bridge over Troubled Water"
19. Music man	He leads the congregation in the Father Rivers response (p. 182). He offers the prayers and the people sing: "God the Father, hear our prayer. Hear us, God the Son. Holy Spirit, hear our prayer. Mercy on your people, Lord." He invites them to offer spontaneous prayers in the silences. The congregation again responds with the chorus. Then he asks them to use this as a time of quiet commitment to build a bridge to someone . . . to reach out to someone . . . to be a healing force in someone's life.	Refer to page 28.
20. Layman	He asks a pre-chosen group from the front to stand and demonstrate the blessing. They touch with both hands as they pass the blessing. John: May the peace of Christ be with you, Helen. Helen: And with your spirit, John. Helen: May the peace of Christ be with you, Paul.	Rehearse this before the service with several people who will sit on the front row. It's lovely, so be sure the people really understand it before you start.††

GOOFS WE MADE: †This service was so long that we cut section 16—offering and all!
††Because the people in back couldn't see what we were doing, some confusion resulted.

SECTION AND RESPONSIBILITY	SCRIPT	ADDENDA
(20., cont.)	Paul: And with your spirit, Helen. Paul: May the peace of . . . Then simultaneously the first person of each row starts the blessing and it passes down the rows.	
21. Music man	He leads the congregation in "Peace, My Friends" (p. 183).	
22. Minister	Benediction	Very tender
23. Music	Repeat "They'll Know We Are Christians by Our Love" (p. 184).	We said: "Would you like to reach out and take your neighbor's hand?" We would have liked to have used "What the World Needs Now" but we didn't want to ask them to sing a new song at the close of the service.

82

I know it sounds corny, Jesus, but I'm lonely

I wasn't going to get lonely any more, and
so I kept very busy. . . . But it's getting dark
again, and I'm alone; honestly, Lord, I'm lonely
as hell.

Why do I feel sorry for myself? There's no
reason why I should be. You're with me, and I
know it. I'll be with other people in a little while.
I know some of them love me very much in their
own way, and I love some of them very much in
mine . . .

. . . Give me patience and love so that I can
listen when I plug into these other lives. Help
me to listen and listen and listen . . . and
love by being quiet and serving, and being there.

—Malcolm Boyd

I've searched for community in many places, Jesus

I was often looking in the wrong places, but
I don't think my motive was altogether wrong. I
was looking futilely and hopelessly there for
fellowship, belonging and acceptance.

Now, . . . I have found community where
and as it is. It seems to me it is your gift.

I am here with these others for only a few *moments*
~~hours~~. I will *soon* be gone ~~tomorrow~~. But I won't be
searching so desperately any more. I know I must
accept community where you offer it to me. I
accept it in this moment. Thank you, Jesus.

—Malcolm Boyd

I Corinthians 13

If I speak with the eloquence of men and of angels, but have no love, I become no more than blaring brass or crashing cymbal. If I have the gift of foretelling the future and hold in my mind not only all human knowledge but the very secrets of God, and if I also have that absolute faith which can move mountains, but have no love, I amount to nothing at all. If I dispose of all that I possess, yes, even if I give my own body to be burned, but have no love, I achieve precisely nothing.

This love of which I speak is slow to lose patience—it looks for a way of being constructive. It is not possessive; it is neither anxious to impress nor does it cherish inflated ideas of its own importance.

Love has good manners and does not pursue selfish advantage. It is not touchy. It does not keep account of evil or gloat over the wickedness of other people. On the contrary, it is glad with all good men when truth prevails.

Love knows no limit to its endurance, no end to its trust, no fading of its hope; it can outlast anything. It is, in fact, the one thing that still stands when all else has fallen.

For if there are prophecies they will be fulfilled and done with, if there are "tongues" the need for them will disappear, if there is knowledge it will be swallowed up in truth. For our knowledge is always incomplete and our prophecy is always incomplete, and when the complete comes, that is the end of the incomplete.

When I was a little child I talked and felt and thought like a little child. Now that I am a man my childish speech and feeling and thought have no further significance for me.

At present we are men looking at puzzling reflections in a mirror. The time will come when we shall see reality whole and face to face! At present all I know is a little fraction of the truth, but the time will come when I shall know it as fully as God now knows me!

In this life we have three great lasting qualities—faith, hope and love. But the greatest of them is love.

—J. B. Phillips' translation

The Good Earth

THE GOOD

EARTH

FATHER RIVERS' RESPONSE

Praise Christ the Son of the Living God.
Glory to God, glory, all praise Him, alleluia.
Glory to God, glory, all praise the name of the Lord.

PEOPLE:
In the beginning God created the heavens and the earth. The
earth was without form and void, and darkness was upon the
face of the deep; and the Spirit of God was moving over the
face of the waters.   READER:
In the beginning of the technological age, man recreated the
heavens and the earth. To the earth he gave new form with
dynamite and bulldozer, and the void of the heavens he filled
with smog.

PEOPLE:
And God said, "Let there be a firmament in the midst of the
waters. . . . Let the waters under the heavens be gathered
into one place, and let the dry land appear."
                              READER:
Then man took oil from beneath the ground and spread it over
the waters, until it coated the beaches with slime. He washed
the topsoil from the fertile prairies and sank it in the
ocean depths. He took waste from his mines and filled in
the valleys, while real estate developers leveled the hills.

PEOPLE: and man said, "Well, business is business."
Then God said, "Let the earth put forth vegetation, plants
yielding seed and fruit trees bearing fruit in which is their
seed, each according to its kind, upon the earth. . . . Let
the earth bring forth living creatures according to their
kinds." And it was so. And God saw that it was good.
                              READER:
But man was not so sure. He found that mosquitoes annoyed him,
so he killed them with DDT. And the robins died, too, and man
said, "What a pity." Man defoliated forests in the name of
modern warfare. He filled the streams with industrial waste--

PEOPLE: and his children read about fishing . . . in the history books.
So God created man in his own image; in the image of God he
created him. And God blessed them, and God said to them,
"Be fruitful and multiply, and fill the earth and subdue it,
and have dominion over . . . every living thing."
                              READER:
So man multiplied--and multiplied--and spread his works across
the land until the last green glade was black with asphalt,
until the skies were ashen and the waters reeked, 'til neither
bird sang not child ran laughing through cool grass. So man
subdued the earth and made it over in his image, and in the
name of progress he drained it of its life . . .
. . . . Until the earth was without form and void, and darkness
was once again upon the face of the deep . . .

87

The Wire Fence

The wires are holding hands around the holes;
To avoid breaking the ring, they hold tight the
neighboring wrist,
And it's thus that with holes they make a fence.

Lord, there are lots of holes in my life.
There are some in the lives of my neighbors.
But if you wish, we shall hold hands,
We shall hold very tight,
And together we shall make a fine roll
of fence to adorn
Paradise.

Michel Quoist

THE GOOD EARTH

THEME: The dual theme of this service is the physical and spiritual pollution of God's world and His people. We look at the problems and seek the solutions.

SECTION AND RESPONSIBILITY	SCRIPT	ADDENDA
1. Art	Set design: pollution banners and posters; trash can at the foot of the Cross with a sign that reads: "Leave your spiritual pollution here."†	This makes a good project for teenagers.
2. Music	Pre-service music on tape: 1. "Nature's Disappearing" (John Mayall; Polydor label, St. George Music, Ltd.) 2. "Yellow Taxi" (Joni Mitchell) 3. "Didn't It Rain, Children" (Evelyn Freeman) 4. "The Hippie Version of Creation" (John Rydgren; Silhouette Segments, Lutheran Church) 5. "His Land" (Ralph Carmichael)	
3. Music man	He leads the singing: 1. "This Land Is Your Land" (p. 184) 2. "God Made the World" (p. 182) 3. "Go Tell It on the Mountain" (p. 182) And teaches the new Father Rivers response (p. 183): 4. "Praise Christ the Son of the Living God; Glory to God, glory, all praise Him, alleluia. Glory to God, glory, all praise the name of the Lord."	
4. Film	Hallelujah film strip from *His Land* (p. 187)	If you rented the film for the first service, you can use the Hallelujah Chorus section here.

GOOFS WE MADE: †The sign should have been on one poster (see photo, p. 89). Preparation was too little and too late!

SECTION AND RESPONSIBILITY	SCRIPT	ADDENDA
5. Drama	"The Creation" by James Weldon Johnson (p. 186)	If possible, invite a black brother to do this one.
6. Film	Film: "Autumn—Frost Country" (p. 187). Robert Frost reading "The Road Not Taken" (New England Visuals, p. 187)†	
7. Music	Solo: "Climb Every Mountain" (p. 182)	
8. Film Sound	Film: "Pollution" (p. 187) Play tape of "The Air" from *Hair* and "Sounds of Pollution" while showing the silent film.	
9. Drama man	He leads the congregation reading "The Sin of Terricide" (pp. 87, 186).	This is a response that compares what God did in creation with what man has done.
10. Layman	He speaks about some of the things that individuals can do in working toward solutions in ecology.	
11. Minister	He invites the offering while a young girl sings a folk song with guitar: "I Built a Garden" (p. 183)	
12. Layman††	He speaks about spiritual pollution—the inner pollution of our own lives. He presents Christ as the solution through the Cross, the Cross being the place where we can bring all our troubles and leave them and be renewed. Jesus said, "Come unto me, all ye who labor and are heavy laden, and I will give you rest." He takes	

GOOFS WE MADE: †We couldn't get the film in time so our film committee came up with a lovely homemade one.
††We leaned too heavily on laymen in this service. It would have been better to use our pastor for more than the offering.

SECTION AND RESPONSIBILITY	SCRIPT	ADDENDA
(12., cont.)	the burden that we may be strengthened through Him, and then minister to others.	
13. Music man	He leads in the new Father Rivers response (p. 92, sec. 3) as the people offer their own prayers during the silences.	
14. Dance	Dancer leads the congregation in movement to "Joy Is Like the Rain" (p. 183). At the end of the song they are reaching out with arms around each other and hold while . . .	The dancer invites the people to follow her movements. Each leader must work out her own design. Just keep it simple: arms uplifted to God, drifting down as the rain, reaching out to each other, touching fingertips, holding hands, swaying, etc. All this can be done with the people standing in their rows if space is limited.
15. Minister Music man	. . . the minister closes in prayer. Before he says "Amen," the music man leads the people in "Kum-by-ya" (p. 183); then the minister says "Amen."	If the people seem to want to keep moving, have them sway as they hold each other during "Kum-by-ya."

The Risk of Caring

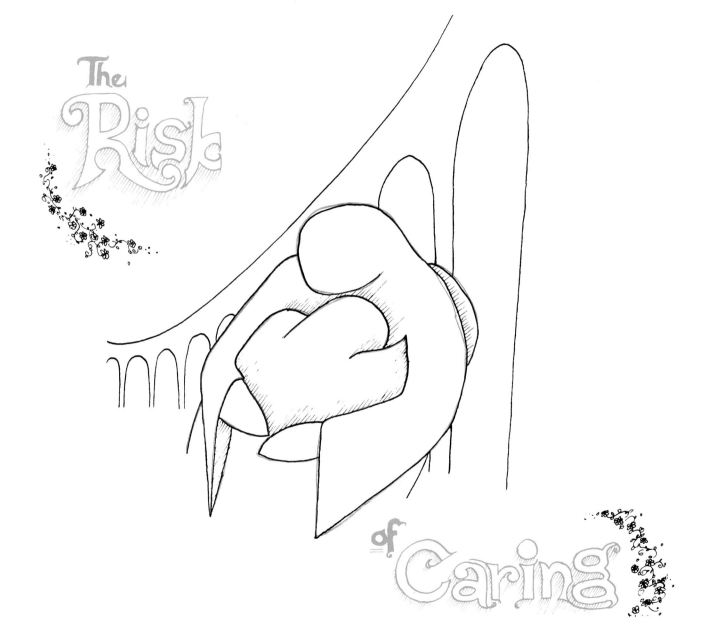

INVOLVEMENT

I have seen a family displaced, with no money, no home
     and no place to go.
I have seen a man broken, humiliated, scorned, for standing
     against what he thought was wrong.
I have seen poor people who are hungry and cold,
     rich people who are desperate and empty.
I have heard the cries of unwanted children, and the longing
     prayers of a woman whose husband doesn't love her any more.

Lord, I stand before you as one who can never say,
"But God, I did not know . . ."
For I know that you mourn for these, your anguished children,
And for us, your complacent children,
And for all your beloved children throughout the earth.

I have seen you suffering in them, Lord.
I have felt you begging us to care.
I have heard you calling us to service.

Because I am aware I am responsible.
Because I am cognizant I am accountable.
Because I would worship you I must comfort them.

For that which I have seen and heard
Has left me
Innocent no more.

TRY A LITTLE KINDNESS

Chorus:
You've got to try a little kindness
Yes, show a little kindness
Just shine your light for everyone to see.
And if you try a little kindness
Then you'll overcome the blindness
Of the narrow-minded people
On the narrow-minded street.

DAY IS DONE

Chorus:
And if you'll take my hand, my son,
All will be well when the day is done.
And if you'll take my hand, my son,
All will be well when the day is done.
Day is done, day is done,
Day is done, day is done.

When men are Animated
by the charity of Christ
they feel united—
And the needs,
Sufferings
and Joys
of others
are felt as
their own.

Pope John

THE RISK OF CARING

THEME: In our city, people are hungry, lonely, sick, and frightened. Jesus said: "Do not turn away from the one who needs your help." Let's take the risk of caring.

SECTION AND RESPONSIBILITY	SCRIPT	ADDENDA
1. Art	Set design: banners and posters with compassion themes	
2. Sound	Pre-service music on tape 1. "The Church Is Burning" (Paul Simon) 2. "Less of Me" (Glenn Campbell) 3. "I'm Going to Lead the Life I Sing about" (Mahalia Jackson) 4. "A Most Peculiar Man" (Paul Simon) 5. "People Who Need People" (Barbra Streisand)	Yes, we know we used Paul Simon twice, but the songs really support the theme.
3. Music	A female singer with guitar leads the congregation in two songs: 1. "Try a Little Kindness" (pp. 97, 184) 2. "Day Is Done" (pp. 98, 182) Then a male soloist sings: 1. "First Corinthians" (an original) 2. "Dakota Hymn" (an Indiana anthem, p. 182)	
4. Drama Music	Scripture: I John 3:17, 18 (p. 107)† Guitar strums in background during reading.	Try a flute or a harp, gently, gently.

GOOFS WE MADE: †It would have been better to have the minister follow the Scripture reading with a short prayer.

SECTION AND RESPONSIBILITY	SCRIPT	ADDENDA
5. Film	Film: "Restricted Neighborhood" (p. 187)	The film shows a young couple who stand up for their principles. They find their "dream house," but don't buy it when they find out that the neighborhood is restricted.
6. Drama Music	Scripture: Matthew 25:35–40 (p. 107) Guitar in background.	
7. Dance	Dance: "Tell It All, Brother" (Kenny Rogers and The First Edition)	
8. Drama Music	The reader leads the people in the congregational reading: "Involvement" (pp. 97, 186). Guitar in background.	
9. Minister	The minister reflects on the theme: There is a cost to involvement, but there is also a cost to noninvolvement.	
10. Layman	He leads the people in some sensitivity experiences that promote interpersonal involvement.†	This is a good spot for a layman with a background in sensitivity. If you don't have someone who knows how to lead this, you may want to invite a psychologist.
11. Music	The soloist leads the people in the response "Lord, make me an Instrument of Your Peace" while the congregation offers spontaneous prayers during the silences.	This is used the same way as the Father Rivers response on page 28 and page 81, section 19.
12. Minister	He invites the offering for a specific ministry (we chose to help a church in the ghetto area).	

GOOFS WE MADE: †This went on too long. If you plan over five minutes per topic, the discussion had better be profound! Also, it should be stated in the introductory remarks that Christ called us to an "in-depth" involvement with others. There's a lot of Scripture for this.

SECTION AND RESPONSIBILITY	SCRIPT	ADDENDA
13. Music	While the young people collect the offering, the soloist sings "He Ain't Heavy, He's My Brother" (p. 182).	
14. Music	Another soloist leads the people in: 1. "No Man Is an Island" (p. 183) 2. "Peace, My Friends" (p. 183) She asks them to hold hands for the benediction.	
15. Minister	The benediction should reinforce the concept of a loving, caring God, and our responsibility to our brother.†	The benediction could start with the reading of "The Wire Fence" (pp. 91, 186).

GOOFS WE MADE: †Wish we had thought of a way to send them out doing something other than singing or just leaving—something that helps them relate to someone else.

I John 3: 17,18

But if any one has the world's goods and sees his brother
in need, yet closes his heart against him, how does God's
love abide in him? Little children, let us not love in
word or speech but in deed and in truth.

Matthew 25:35—40

For I was hungry and you gave me food, I was thirsty and
you gave me drink, I was a stranger and you welcomed me,
I was naked and you clothed me, I was sick and you visited
me, I was in prison and you came to me.' Then the righteous
will answer him, 'Lord, when did we see thee hungry and
feed thee, or thirsty and give thee drink? And when did
we see thee a stranger and welcome thee, or naked and
clothe thee? And when did we see thee sick or in prison
and visit thee?' And the King will answer them, 'Truly,
I say to you, as you did it to one of the least of these
my brethren, you did it to me.'

—Revised Standard Version

Man For All Seasons

Man For
All Seasons

MAN FOR ALL SEASONS

READER:
He came in a certain time and a certain place
With a love that could not be contained in a given
        time, at a given place.
He came in one season--for all seasons,
He died one death for all deaths.
He came that we might have life--
        and have it more abundantly.

RESPONSE:
Lord, I want to be a Christian in my heart.

And he said at one time
What was meant for all times:
"Come to me, all who labor and are heavy laden, and
I will give you rest. Take my yoke upon you, and
learn from me; for I am gentle and lowly in heart,
and you will find rest for your souls. For my
yoke is easy, and my burden is light."

Lord, I want to be a Christian in my heart.

"Ask, and it will be given you;
Seek, and you will find;
Knock, and the door will be opened to you."

Lord, I want to be a Christian in my heart.

"Do not lay up for yourselves treasures on earth,
where moth and rust consume and where thieves break
in and steal, but lay up for yourselves treasures
in heaven, where neither moth nor rust consumes
and where thieves do not break in and steal.
For where your treasure is, there will your
heart be also.

Lord, I want to be a Christian in my heart.

"Anyone who has seen me has seen the Father . . .
for I am the way, the truth, and the life . . .
lo, I am with you always, even to the end of
time . . . I came that your joy might be full . . ."

Lord, I want to be a Christian in my heart.

"For God so loved the world that he gave his only
Son, that whoever believes in him should not
perish but have eternal life. For God sent the
Son into the world, not to condemn the world,
but that the world might be saved through him."

Lord, I want to be a Christian in my heart.

111

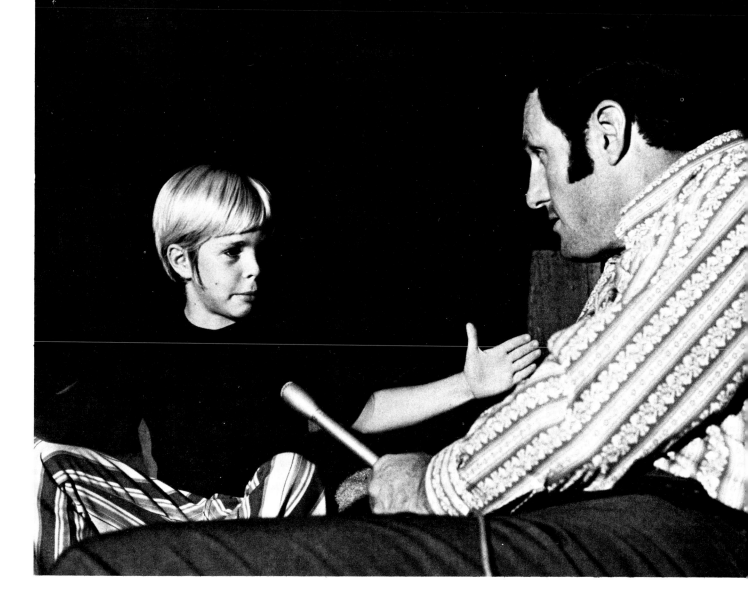

MAN FOR ALL SEASONS

THEME: We explore the many facets of Jesus the man and Jesus the Messiah. We share the uniqueness of our individual relationship with Him.

SECTION AND RESPONSIBILITY	SCRIPT	ADDENDA
1. Art	Set design: Christ-centered banners	
2. Music Sound	Pre-service music on tape: 1. "Jesus Christ, Superstar" (Tim Rice, Andre Lloyd Webber) 2. "I Am the Resurrection" (Ray Repp) 3. "O Lamb of God" (David Yantis) 4. "Lord, I Want to Be a Christian" (Evelyn Freeman) 5. "Put Your Hand in the Hand" (Ocean)	
3. Music man Music	He leads the congregation in two songs: 1. "Here Comes Jesus" (p. 182) 2. "Ride On, King Jesus" (p. 183) A soloist sings: "The Man" (p. 183)	
4. Layman	A member of the college department introduces himself and tells about a film he made. He explains that this was a personal expression of his faith. We see his film: "In the Presence of the Lord."	He matched the film to the rock record "In the Presence of the Lord" ("Blind Faith," Atco) and produced a contemporary statement of faith.
5. Music man	The music man introduces the guest musicians (a folk-rock group of Jesus people). They play for ten minutes and share short statements of what Jesus means to them.	It's fun to invite professional or semiprofessional groups. (Once we didn't hear the group before we asked them to come. Recommend you never, never do that!)
6. Minister	The pastor talks about the different concepts that people have of Jesus. He invites the people to share in a few sentences their feelings and insights. What is He to them?	This takes great sensitivity and openness to allow for the differences in people's levels of faith. Give them the freedom to express even their lack of faith, if that's where they are.

SECTION AND RESPONSIBILITY	SCRIPT	ADDENDA
7. Drama	A storyteller tells a child's story with adult appeal.	This was an original story—seek ye a resident poet!
8. Music	The folk-rock group plays for ten minutes.† The selections continue to present the many facets of Jesus' life and influence.	
9. Drama man Music man	He reads "Man for All Seasons" (p. 111) from the program while the congregation sings the response.	
10. Minister	The minister invites the offering and offers a short prayer.	
11. Music	While the gifts are being collected, a soloist sings "The Man for Me" (p. 183)	
12. Minister	Drawing from the people's statements in section 6, he weaves a short, extemporaneous message, summing up with the scriptural answer to the question "What is He to me?"	This kind of improvisational freedom comes easily to some, not so easily to others. Try it and trust; it's the very essence of creative worship.
13. Music Music man	The folk-rock group plays a closing song and the music man starts them singing "Amen" (p. 182) on the way out.††	

GOOFS WE MADE: †Encouraged by our enthusiasm, the group played so long we had to cut section 9.
††We should have chosen a more gentle song since the congregation felt pensive and quiet. "Amen" works well at the end of an exuberant service.

Expressions of Love—
Candlelight Communion

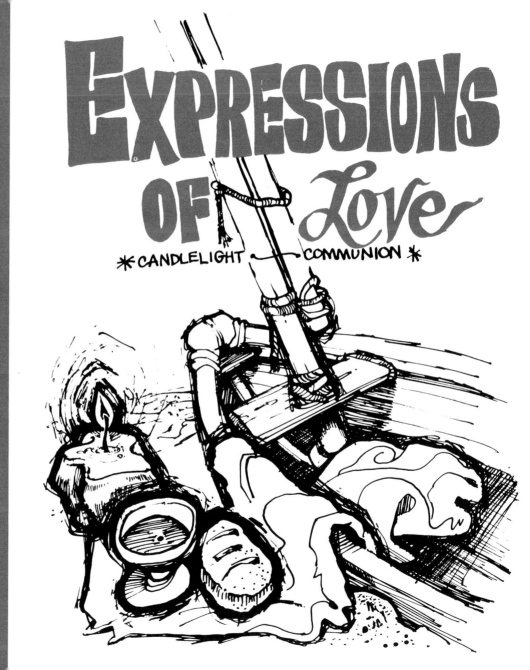

EXPRESSIONS OF Love

CANDLELIGHT COMMUNION

Renewal

You asked for my hands that You could use them for Your Purpose.
I gave them for a moment and then withdrew for the work was hard.

You asked for my mouth to speak out against injustice.
I gave You a whisper that I might not be accused.

You asked for my eyes to see the pain of poverty.
I closed them for I did not want to know.

You asked for my life that You might work through me.
I gave You a fractional part that I might not get involved.

Lord, forgive me for calculated efforts to serve you only
        when it is convenient to do so,
Only in places where it is safe to do so,
Only with those who make it easy to do so.
Father, forgive me, renew me, and send me out as a
        usable instrument,
That I may take seriously the meaning of
                Your cross.

The Holy Communion is the Creator's act
through his people of binding
the wounds and healing
a broken humanity. Sometimes
it is a party. Sometimes it is not.
But participation in it signals your
desire to take on hope.
Therefore all people confessing
their frail humanity and
yearning for a greater are
welcome to come to the altar and
receive the
Holy Communion.

Corita Kent

EXPRESSIONS OF LOVE

THEME: We come to the Lord's table, confessing our frail humanity, seeking renewal and rededicating our lives.

SECTION AND RESPONSIBILITY	SCRIPT	ADDENDA
1. Art	Set design: communion and joy banners; a burlap cover on the communion table; clay chalice and pitcher, sand candles, home-baked bread.	Consult a potter for the chalices (or a specialty shop); ask your teenagers to make sand candles; ask the women's association to bake the bread.
2. Music	Pre-service music on tape 1. "God Is Real" (Mahalia Jackson) 2. "Amazing Grace" (Joni Mitchell) 3. "Peace, My Friends" (Ray Repp) 4. "The Wedding Song" (Paul Stookey)	
3. Music man	He leads ten minutes of congregational singing: 1. "He's Got the Whole World in His Hands" (p. 182) 2. "Come before the Table of the Lord" (p. 182) 3. "But Then Comes the Morning" (p. 182)	This service is low key and gentle; use candlelight if possible.†
4. Drama	"Creed" (pp. 129, 186)	Readers come from their places in the congregation; several microphones are needed in large situations. Let all the service happen from among the people—not from the pulpit. Remember, don't introduce readers or singers—their participation almost appears to be spontaneous.

GOOFS WE MADE: †Honestly, we just don't feel there were any goofs in this service.

SECTION AND RESPONSIBILITY	SCRIPT	ADDENDA
5. Drama	"Tied" (pp. 130, 186)	
6. Music	Choir: "Ave Verum Corpus" (communion anthem by Mozart, p. 182)	In a contemporary worship service, a well-chosen classic can be most effective.
7. Music	"Hymn" (p. 183)	
8. Minister	He leads the congregational reading "Renewal" (pp. 121, 186).	
9. Music man	He leads the congregation in "Let Us Break Bread Together" (p. 183).	
10. Minister	He explains the meaning of communion, gives the invitation to the table, and explains the procedure outlined in the Addenda.	Three elders or ministers come forward and take a tray from the communion table, which has been set with a clay pitcher of wine, a clay chalice, and a loaf of home-baked bread on a red napkin. They proceed to three tables in the back or sides of the sanctuary and kneel around low tables covered with burlap and sand candles. The people come to the table at any time throughout the rest of the service. They kneel, hold hands, pray, and serve each other. The bread is dipped in the wine. The minister could incorporate the reading by Corita Kent, page 125.
11. Music	Baroque instruments play selections from Bach.	From this point on, music and readings alternate while the people come to the table when they feel ready. The flow of people, directed only by the Holy Spirit, in no way distracts from the worship.
12. Drama	Spiritual graffiti: 1. "One Solitary Life" (p. 131) 2. "Backwards" (pp. 132, 186) 3. "Eight" (pp. 133, 186)	

SECTION AND RESPONSIBILITY	SCRIPT	ADDENDA
13. Music	Solo: "My Sweet Lord" (p. 183)	
14. Drama	"You Are like the Noonday Sun in the Night" (pp. 133, 186)	
15. Drama	Hasidic Story (p. 131)	
16. Music	Choir: "Pass It On" (p. 183)	The music man must be prepared to add more music if the people are still taking communion. "Pass It On" concludes the Lord's Supper section of the service.
17. Drama	"Benediction" (pp. 134, 186)	
18. Minister	An intimate prayer.	
19. Dance Music Minister	The dancer leads the people in movement to "Peace, My Friends" (p. 183). The service closes as they stand with arms around each other, swaying and singing. The minister offers the benediction as the people hum the refrain.	See "The Good Earth" Addenda, section 14.

Creed

The Apostles' Creed is old and I say it only on Sundays. But it has a weekday feeling to me.

It was good the way we said the creed today. Slow. Slow enough to think and for everyone to say weekday words in between the old sentences.

I believe in the forgiveness of sin

for janitors who take dope and jump down your neck
for community leaders apprehended by the law
for people who spread rumors
for those who slam down phones
for people who transfer when they are mad
for those who read religious publications
for proud professors
for murderers
for bullies
for prostitutes
for priests and pastors
for my son.

I believe in the resurrection of the body

for people I can't stand
for those who criticize my work
for beauty queens
for my mother and father
for myself.

I am a believer, Lord, I do believe.

—Herbert F. Brokering

129

Tied

The ushers had no bulletins.

The ushers had two pieces of rope per two people.

We sat two by two, tied to one another. Tied by foot and tied by hand. United, bound, joined by hand and foot.

Two by two by two by two we sat in every pew. As one stood the other stood. As one walked the other walked. As one knelt the other knelt.

We were conscious of every motion. There was always another in the same act. Nothing was singular or automatic.

I went to the communion table. We both went. No one could go alone. Together we confessed, ate, drank, walked, knelt, stood, sang, and prayed.

The pile of rope beside the ushers was a sign of a very extraordinary hour of communal living.

Some debated the technique. Some had nothing to say. For some there was nothing left to say. It is doubtful that anyone has forgotten the hour.

The rope hangs over my desk. The man to whom I was tied is on my mind.

—Herbert F. Brokering

One Solitary Life

He was born in an obscure village, the child of a peasant woman. He grew up in still another village, where he worked in a carpenter shop until he was thirty. Then for three years he was an itinerant preacher. He never held office. He never had a family or owned a house. He didn't go to college. He never visited a big city. He never traveled two hundred miles from the place where he was born. He did none of the things one usually associates with greatness. He had no credentials but himself. He was only thirty-three when the tide of public opinion turned against him. His friends ran away. He was turned over to his enemies and went through the mockery of a trial. He was nailed to a cross between two thieves. While he was dying, his executioners gambled for his clothing, the only property he had on earth. When he was dead, he was laid in a borrowed grave through the pity of a friend. Nineteen centuries have come and gone, and today he is the central figure of the human race and the leader of mankind's progress. All the armies that ever marched, all the navies that ever sailed, all the parliaments that ever sat, all the kings that ever reigned, put together, have not affected the life of man on this earth as much as that **one solitary life.**

—Anonymous

Hasidic Story

A little farmer boy, having been left an orphan at an early age, was unable to read, but had inherited a large, heavy prayer book from his parents. On the Day of Atonement he brought it into the synagogue, laid it on the reading desk, and, weeping, cried out: "Lord of Creation! I do not know how to pray; I do not know what to say—I give Thee the entire prayer book."

Backwards

The people no longer heard the prayer. They'd said it so many times. He said it backwards and they wondered where he'd learned it. And they learned to say it forwards again.

Father, yours is the glory.
Father, yours is the power.
Father, yours is the kingdom.
Father, deliver us from evil;
   lead us not into temptation;
    forgive us our debts, as we forgive our debtors;
    give us this day our daily bread.
Father, your will be done on earth, as it is in heaven;
   your kingdom come;
   hallowed be your name.
In heaven.
Our Father.
Amen.

—Herbert F. Brokering

Eight

Clouds are not the cheeks of angels you know
they're only clouds.
          Friendly sometimes,
but you can never be sure.
If I had longer arms
I'd push the clouds away
or make them hang above the water somewhere else,
but I'm just a man
          who needs and wants,
mostly things he'll never have.
Looking for that thing that's hardest to find—

I've been going a long time now
along the way I've learned some things.
          You have to make the good times yourself
take the little times and make them into big times
and save the times that are all right
          for the ones that aren't so good.

I've never been able
          to push the clouds away by myself.
               Help me.
Please.

—Rod McKuen,
Listen to the Warm

You Are Like
the Noonday Sun in the Night

O Lord, Creator.
Ruler of the world, Father,
I thank, thank, thank you
that you have brought me through.
How strong the pain was—
but you were stronger.
How deep the fall was—
but you were even deeper.
How dark was the night—
but you were the noonday sun in it.
You are our father,
our mother.
our brother, and our friend.
Your grace has no end,
and your light no snuffer.
We praise you,
we honor you,
and we pray to your holy name.
We thank you
that you rule thus,
and that you are so merciful
with your tired followers.
Praised be you
through our Lord Jesus Christ.
Amen.

—From *I Lie on My Mat and Pray*
Prayers by Young Africans

Benediction

The ushers had the doors waiting. In thirty seconds the people would
be leaving, they figured.
It was longer today. The pastor surprised his people.
He said the Benediction, interjecting Out there! throughout.

> The Lord bless you and keep you, out there!
> The Lord make his face to shine upon you and
>   be gracious unto you, out there!
> The Lord lift up his countenance upon you
>   and give you peace, out there!

Out there! he said. And we left for our farms and suburbs and cities,
blessed. It was like scattering the Benediction into the restaurants, jails,
cars, elevators, kitchens, theaters, science labs, sports arenas, back
yards, honeymoon motels, playgrounds, and family dinners.

I went fishing. I knew I had the Benediction in my boat.

My boy went back to boot camp. He knew he had the Benediction
in his bunk.

—Herbert F. Brokering

III. Two Giant Sized Happenings

A Celebration of Evangelism • A Revolution of Love
Cincinnati, Ohio - 1971 -

Catch the New Wind

A Celebration of Evangelism
A Revolution of Love

And the People sing—

From the voices of children, Lord
comes the _sound_ of your praise.

God the Father, hear our prayer.
Hear us God, the Son
Holy Spirit, hear our prayer.
Mercy on Your people, Lord.

Come on people now
Smile on your brother
Everybody get together
Try to love one another
Right now!

I have nothing at all without love
There are but three things that last:
Faith, Hope—Faith, Hope and Love,
But the greatest of these is Love.

Glo (ho-ho) re (hee)
glo (ho-ho) re (hee)
glory, sing to the Lord

God made the world:
Everything is good
Everything He's made
Shouts His Praise.

Singers: Skip Sanders
• Paul Bergen
• The Young Folk directed by Harry
• West Cincinnati Mission Causey
Church Children's Choir directed by
Sylvia Hunter

Dancers:
• Marge Champion
• John West
• Sacred Dance Group
from the Forest Chapel
United Methodist Church

Musicians:
• Jack Miffleton
• Neil Blunt
• Louise Anderson

Banners:
• Jean Pegram
• Gloria Wood
Forest Chapel
United Methodist
Church
Beverly Hills
Community Presbyterian
Church

Poet:
• Marilee Ydenek

Program Graphics:
• Ron Riddick

Leaders:
• Gary Demarest
• Bruce Larson

Directors:
• Marilee Ydenek
• Marge Champion

140

CATCH THE NEW WIND

SECTION AND PARTICIPANTS	SCRIPT	ADDENDA	SPECIAL EQUIPMENT
1. Jean Pegram Margaret Dickason	Set design: The room is covered with thirty joy banners and paper hangings. The stage is dressed with two balloon trees and six banners. Fifteen balloon trees bank the walls of the room.	Get professional help for lights and mikes. Fill balloons with air and helium.	3,000 daisies 3,000 balloons 15 balloon trees 2 helium tanks 2 air compressors masking tape yarn to tie balloons
2. Harry Causey	The Young Folk: Fifty teenagers bank both sides of the entrance and sing for twenty minutes while the people "walk through" before entering the room. Some of The Young Folk are passing out programs; some are located on the stairway and giving everyone who comes in a daisy. They are casually dressed in maxis, minis, or jeans.	Musical selections included: "Put Your Hand in the Hand" "Alle-Alle" "I'm on My Way" "Get Together" "Peace I Leave with You"	Four microphones outside the room pipe the music into the main sound system.
3. Harry Causey	Processional: The group enters singing "When the Saints Go Marching in" (p. 184), weaving in and out of the rows and finally sitting along the steps of the stage and on the floor. (300 center chairs have been removed to let some of the people sit on the floor.)		
4. Rev. Gary Demarest	Call to Worship: Gary has been sitting on the floor; now he stands and offers the call to worship from the midst of the people.	No tie, remember?	Hand mike on 50-foot cord.

SECTION AND PARTICIPANTS	SCRIPT	ADDENDA	SPECIAL EQUIPMENT
5. Skip Sanders, music man Father Jack Miffleton, guitar Father Neil Blunt, guitar Louise Anderson, bass Paul Sketch, drums Mike Bobbitt, lead guitar	The people sing: 1. Solo: "O Happy Day" (p. 183) 2. Congregation: "God Made the World" (pp. 139, 182) 3. Congregation: "Glory" (pp. 139, 182) 4. Solo: "You've Got a Friend" (p. 184) 5. Congregation: "Come before the Table of the Lord" (p. 182)		5 standing microphones bank of lights hung from ceiling 2 spotlights with surprise pink gelatines
6. Skip Sanders Marilee Zdenek	The New Wind: Skip starts "The New Wind" (pp. 147-48) and is joined by Marilee and Paul (a reading with cantor)		
7. Paul Bergen	The Apostle's Creed Paul sings blues rendition of creed (p. 182), accompanied by drums	Be sure microphones are cleared for the dancers.	
8. Marge Champion John West Sacred Dance Group, Forest Hill Chapel Methodist Church	Liturgical dance: Marge, John, and the Methodist dancers praise God with dance: "The Lord's Prayer" (Barbra Streisand recording)		Tape deck, record transferred to tape
9. Skip Sanders Paul Bergen	Prayer and response: Skip teaches the "God the Father" response (pp. 139, 182) and Paul sings the intercessions.		
10. Rev. Bruce Larson	Sensitivity: Bruce involves the people in a gentle, sensitivity interaction.		
11. Skip Sanders	The people sing (with Skip): 1. "Let's Get Together" (pp. 139, 183)		

	2. "From the Voices of Children" (pp. 139, 182)		
12. West Cincinnati Children's Choir	Guest choir: 1. "Certainly, Lord" 2. "Hello, Sunshine" 3. "I Know the Lord"	When you invite a group, you go with their selections.	
13. Rev. Gary Demarest	The Parable of the Balloon: Gary tells the "Parable of the Balloon" (p. 63). Taking a balloon, he taps it to one of the children, showing that the balloon is like a blessing and that we cannot force it on another. He involves a couple of people near the stage as he explains that our evangelism should be gentle like the balloon, that we should send out our blessings but leave it to God where they go, as they are blown by the Wind of the Spirit.		
The Young Folk	The teenagers fan out across the room to release the balloons from the trees and tap them to the people as they share a blessing: God loves you; have a happy day; etc.		
Skip Sanders	Skip sings "The Spirit Is a-Movin'" (p. 184).		
14. Marge Champion The Young Folk	Congregational movement: Marge leads the people in movement as The Young Folk sing "Joy Is like the Rain" (p. 183).		
15. Rev. Gary Demarest Paul Bergen Skip Sanders	As the people are standing with arms around each other, Gary closes in prayer with the benediction; everyone sings "Amen" (p. 182).		

The New Wind

SKIP: (SINGS GENTLY)   THERE IS A NEW WIND BLOWIN'
         (STRONGER)   THERE IS A NEW WIND HERE

Marilee: There is a new wind blowing, born of a need that many
         Christians feel. The new wind blows across the city today,
         and finds its poets, and artists, and musicians, and calls
         them to use their talents to praise God. The wind blows
         across the past, into the early Christian Church, and sweeps
         their excitement and spontaneity right into the Twentieth Century.
         The wind blows through all the nations of the earth, and
         the ethnic variety becomes a symbol of our oneness in Christ.
         With men of all cultures, all races, we praise God in a
         combination of very old and very new forms of worship.

SKIP: (STRONG)   THERE IS A NEW WIND BLOWIN'

Marilee: And the wind will not be stilled, for the faith of the
         worshipers is strong, and the authority for their worship forms
         comes from the Source.

PAUL: (STRONG)   SING TO THE LORD A NEW SONG
SKIP: (ECHO)   THERE IS A NEW WIND NOW . . .

Marilee: Let's celebrate the joy of our faith, and catch the
         New Wind, together.

PAUL: PRAISE HIM WITH LOUD CLASHING CYMBALS

Marilee: Praise Him with cymbals, and guitars, and drums--
         How can one instrument be secular, and another sacred?
         John Calvin destroyed some of the finest organs in
         Switzerland because he thought an organ was too secular for a church.

PAUL: MAKE A JOYFUL NOISE UNTO THE LORD

Marilee: Praise Him with electronic sound, with folk and rock--
         with Renaissance instruments, primitive African instruments,
         maracas, or a flute--

PAUL: (PLAYFULLY)   KING DAVID DANCED BEFORE THE LORD WITH ALL HIS
         MIGHT--LET THE PEOPLE PRAISE HIS NAME WITH DANCING,
         PRAISE HIM WITH TIMBREL AND DANCE

Marilee: Why should we use only our voices for praising?
         Shouldn't the soloist sometimes be a dancer?
         The Hebrew people danced to their God, and the early Christians--
         Why did the church ever stop dancing?

PAUL: MAN LOOKS ON THE OUTWARD APPEARANCES, BUT GOD LOOKS ON THE HEART
LET THE CHILDREN COME UNTO ME

Marilee: Wouldn't you love to go to a church where barefoot, blue-jeaned children could sit on the floor and really be comfortable in their Father's house?

PAUL: (TENDERLY, COMFORTING) COME UNTO ME, ALL YE WHO ARE WEARY AND HEAVY LADEN . . .

Marilee: Sometimes we're weary and lonely. Sometimes we feel like no one really cares, and even our prayers seem to drift off into silence.

PAUL: (SOFTLY) AND JESUS TOUCHED HIM AND HE WAS HEALED

Marilee: Did you ever want to reach out and touch someone, to feel-- comforted, and less alone?

PAUL: (BUILDING) AND JESUS TOUCHED HIM AND HE WAS HEALED

Marilee: Once during communion we held hands . . .

PAUL: AND JESUS TOUCHED HIM AND HE WAS HEALED
AND THE HOLY SPIRIT CAME UPON THEM

Marilee: Suddenly we were touched by joy, and the world was beautiful.

PAUL: GOD DOES NOT LIVE IN HOUSES MADE BY MEN

Marilee: So let's have communion at dawn on the desert,
Find a lake and name it Galilee,
Meet by the sea, and as a congregation, praise Him with flying kites and balloons!

PAUL: (JOYFULLY) PRAISE THE LORD, YOU FLYING BIRDS

Marilee: Let's praise Him with shouts of joy, and whispers of longings and adore Him with an effervescent faith, for God does not delight in our solemnity, and where the Spirit of the Lord is, there is Freedom.

PAUL: THEY WHO WAIT FOR THE LORD SHALL RENEW THEIR STRENGTH,
THEY SHALL RISE UP WITH WINGS LIKE EAGLES
THEY SHALL RUN AND NOT BE WEARY
THEY SHALL WALK AND NOT FAINT . . .

I BELIEVE IN GOD THE FATHER ALMIGHTY . . . (INTO CREED)

God Gives His People Strength
— Candlelight Communion

"I came that you might have life and have it more abundantly!

Forgive, Lord, forgive.
It was night when we did what we did
But then comes the morning
  yesterday's sorrows behind.
Wake, it's the day of your longing,
  Life returns, mercy comes,
        it's morning

God the Father, hear our prayer.
Hear us, God the Son.
Holy Spirit, hear our prayer.
Mercy on Your people, Lord.

Cum-by-ya, my Lord,
cum-by-ya.   Oh, Lord
        Cum-'by-ya

We are one in the Spirit,
        We are one in the Lord,
We are one in the Spirit,
        We are one in the Lord,
And we pray that our Unity may one day
        be restored.
(chorus:)
And they'll know we are Christians
        by our Love,
        by our Love,
Yes, they'll know we are Christians
        by our Love.

We're called to be that city,
We're called to be that city,
We're called to be that city,
We're called to be that light.

Let us break bread together on our knees.
Let us break bread together on our knees,
  when I fall on my knees,
  with my face to the rising sun
Oh, Lord have mercy on me.

151

Directors:
- Marilee Zdenek
- Marge Champion

Leaders:
- Donn Moomaw
- Jerry Kirk

Singers:
- Paul Berger
- Ruth McClain

Dance:
- Marge Champion
- John West

Musicians:
- Jack Miffleton
- Neil Blunt

Program Graphics:
- Ron Riddick

Banners: Jean Pegram • Gloria Wood • Forest Chapel United Methodist Church
- Beverly Hills Community Presbyterian Church

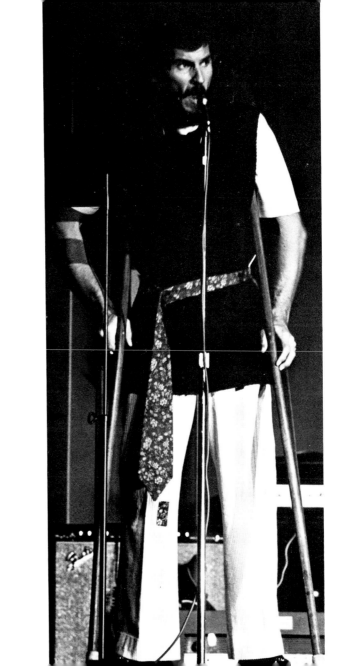

GOD GIVES HIS PEOPLE STRENGTH

SECTION AND PARTICIPANTS	SCRIPT	ADDENDA	SPECIAL EQUIPMENT
1. Jean Pegram Bob Ramey	Set design: A long, low table on the platform, covered with a burlap cloth, is set with earthy communion elements—sand candles, a clay chalice, pitcher of wine, a round loaf of home-baked bread, and a red napkin. Additional tables on each side of the platform hold the elements for the congregation.	The sound problems are complex. They include microphones set in the congregation. Get professional help for this and for lighting. We recommend either still white Catawba, colored with red food coloring, or wine, instead of the traditional grape juice.	15 subdued light fixtures resembling old-fashioned street lights are located around the room. A bank of lights hangs from the ceiling. Two spotlights have surprise pink gelatines.
2. Pat Ellis, harpsichord Bob Gifford, flute	Renaissance music: Soft, gentle music is being played on the electric harpsichord and flute while the people are being seated. Programs are passed out at the door.	A college music department or conservatory of music can help you find qualified performers.	
3. Barbara Murphy, soloist	Opening song: "I Don't Know How to Love Him" (Mary's song from *Jesus Christ, Superstar*, p. 183)		
4. Rev. Donn Moomaw	Prayer: "Lord, we do love you; yet none of us **really** knows how to love . . ."		
5. Paul Bergen, soloist Father Jack Miffleton, guitar Louise Anderson, bass	The people sing: 1. Solo: "Swing Low, Sweet Chariot" (p. 184) 2. Solo and congregation: "We're Called to Be That City" (p. 184) 3. Solo: "Were You There" (p. 184)		

SECTION AND PARTICIPANTS	SCRIPT	ADDENDA	SPECIAL EQUIPMENT
6. Readers: Murray Marshall Jo Ann Yinger Bob Dickson Peggy Bell Rev. John C. Reid	Spiritual graffiti: 1. "Tied" (pp. 130, 186) 2. "Creed," story form (pp. 129, 186) 3. Scripture: Luke 7:40–47 4. "Renewal" (pp. 121, 186) 5. Scripture: I John I	The flute plays softly in the background throughout the readings. Use a modern translation for the Scripture.	4 standing mikes scattered widely in the congregation.
7. Marge Champion John West	Liturgical dance: Marge and John call the people to confession with the dance: "Tell It All, Brother" (Kenny Rogers, and The First Edition)		Pretape music; amplify from tape deck.
8. Rev. Jerry Kirk Rev. Donn Moomaw	Sharing: the role of servant Jerry shares an experience that was a crossroad in his ministry. Donn reads John 13:1–14 from *Good News for Modern Man*. During the Scripture, if Jerry feels led by the Holy Spirit, he will begin the service of footwashing. The music will continue as planned after the Scripture reading.	The Holy Spirit led others to participate at this point. Although footwashing is an unfamiliar element to most Protestants, it was a tender and moving experience and a great force of reconciliation.	
9. Ruth McLain	And the people sing: Ruth sings 2 solos with dulcimer 1. "Twenty-third Psalm" (p. 184) 2. "Consolation" (p. 182) 3. Soloist and congregation: "But Then Comes the Morning" (pp. 151, 182)		
10. Paul Bergen Rev. Robert B. Munger Marilee Zdenek Rev. Howard C. Blake Rev. Louis H. Evans, Jr.	Prayer and response: Paul leads the congregation in the "God the Father" response while four people offer prayers from the congregation.	For details on this refer to "Walls Come Tumbling Down," section 19, and "Straight from the Source," page 28.	

155

SECTION AND PARTICIPANTS	SCRIPT	ADDENDA	SPECIAL EQUIPMENT
11. Rev. Donn Moomaw	Invitation to communion: Donn invites the people to communion and then leads them in singing "Let Us Break Bread Together on Our Knees" (pp. 151, 183). He takes the bread and the chalice and begins the communion at the low table on the platform, where the moderators and several others are kneeling (they have come forward during the song). As they pass the elements they say something personal as they serve each other at the table.	These are the moderators of the five major Presbyterian denominations: Presbyterian Church, U.S. United Presbyterian Church Reform Church in America Cumberland Pres. Church Associate Reformed Presbyterian Church	Long table Burlap cover Sand candles 1 clay chalice 1 pitcher of wine 1 loaf of round bread
Ben Rose Lois Stair Christian Walvoord Thach Shauf Roy Beckham			
12. Rev. Donn Moomaw	The people's communion: Donn asks those who are serving to come forward. Sixty people (twenty serving units) offer the elements to the people. Music continues during the communion.		Long tables in rear 30 trays for bread 300 loaves
Ruth McClain, soloist Pat Ellis, harpsichord Bob Gifford, flute Paul Bergen Moderators	Solo: "God Gives His People Strength" (p. 182) Paul leads "Kum-by-ya" (p. 183) as those at the table say in one word what they are feeling. The people respond, singing, "Bob feels gentle, Lord, Kum-by-ya"—"Helen feels loving, Lord, Kum-by-ya."		
13. Paul Bergen	And the people sing: Paul leads the people in "They'll Know We Are Christians by Our Love" (p. 184), brought down to a hum for the closing prayer (by Donn) and then up again as they go out singing.		
Rev. Donn Moomaw			

IV. Developing Talent Pools

a camel is a horse
that a committee
put together

Let's involve the maximum number of people in Creativity—
(But spend the minimum amount of time in committee meetings.)

It can be done like this:

The basic committee designs the celebration,

ART

MUSIC

DANCE

MINISTER

*DIRECTOR of Creative Worship

LIGHT and SOUND

FILM

DRAMA

✱ for the sake of mental health, give the director a secretary—or production manager or a road-runner or something!

If you can swing it
this will save your **sanity**:

each member
of the basic
committee
directs his own
talent pool

Publicity,
bulletins,
banners,
special effects.

ART

DANCE
A group willing to
be used
throughout the
series.

Select scripture, Provide secretarial help, Research what other churches are doing.

MINISTER

Determine what equipment is needed, set it up — mikes, lighting etc...

LIGHT & SOUND

FILM
Use commercial films and slides — create your own!

BASIC COMMITTEE

DRAMA
Read Scripture, research available talent, do improvisations.

MUSIC
Solos, groups, congregational singing.

If you have a small church! you can *get* by with just the basic committee. However, the talent pools are a good way to get lots of people involved without having total confusion at the basic planning meetings.

Remember! All elements to be used must be co-ordinated by the Creative Worship Director

Carve this
in stone:
everything takes
twice as long to do as
it seems like it should.

For a September series:
start work in June (THIS IS NOT A
TYPOGRAPHICAL ERROR)
unless of course, you are
planning to really USE
those worksheets.

otherwise:

June:
- form committees
- determine themes for all services
- hassle about who is really qualified to do what
- pray a lot (really!)
- relax and figure September is a long way off

July:
- determine major elements that are to be used
- spell out firmly who is to be responsible for what

August: — make detailed work sheets
- dance and drama people start rehearsals
- start publicity

— pray some more) *This* is His show, remember?

September:

 — half-hour before service:
 — have everything ready
   and so <u>**NOW**</u>

 ■ really give it to God—to
   His Glory and for His
   Purpose,

and have the freedom to hang loose
   and let the Spirit take it where
   He will—

(He may turn that work-sheet upside down

— if He doesn't-ever-start worrying... (better yet

NEW DIMENSIONS IN WORSHIP
6:00 p.m.

October 4:   LET THERE BE JOY
October 11:   TREASURE HUNT--THE SERENDIPITIES OF GOD
October 18:   WALLS COME TUMBLING DOWN
October 25:   THE GOOD EARTH
November 1:   THE RISK OF CARING
November 8:   MAN FOR ALL SEASONS
November 15:   EXPRESSIONS OF LOVE--CANDLELIGHT COMMUNION

* * * * * * * *

Tap your talent early—

I would like to help with these services:

_____ 1. Art		_____ 8. Publicity
_____ 2. Music		_____ 9. Secretarial
_____ 3. Dance		_____ 10. Road Runner
_____ 4. Drama		_____ 11. Research
_____ 5. Reading Scripture		_____ 12. Special Talents
_____ 6. Ushering & Offering		_____ 13. Strobe Lights
_____ 7. Electronics & Projection		_____ 14. Other - specify

Original material is welcome!

My special interests are:
(Please be as specific as possible about what you would like to do,
what experience you have had, special talents, etc.)

I would like to work: regularly_____occasionally_____
     teens:_____   20's_____   30's_____   or plus:_____

Name_____

Address_____

Telephone: Home_____Office_____Best hours to call_____

168

V. Creating Banners

use felt, burlap, velvet, and patchwork

Hot colors in unreal combinations

braids and sequins baubles and beads

Banners

Ask the ladies of the sewing circle to turn on all their creativity and praise Him with the work of their hands

Paper hangings are great too. How about 15 feet tall!

Let the banners support the theme

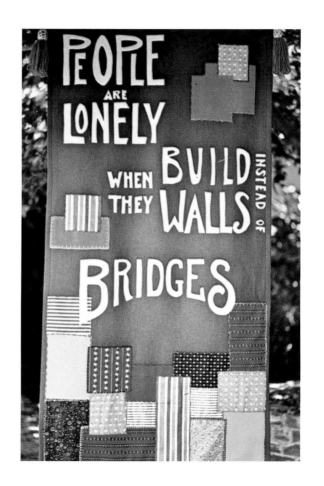

174

WHERE THE SPIRIT OF THE LORD IS THERE IS FREEDOM

2 COR 3:17

175

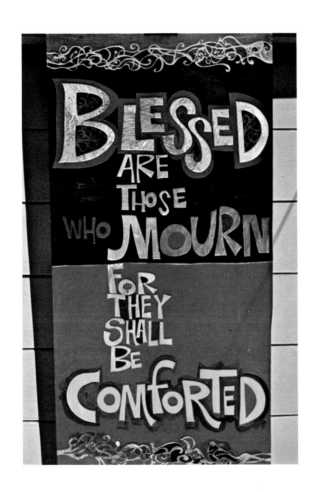

179

VI. Making the Most of Existing Material

MAKING THE MOST OF EXISTING MATERIALS

MUSIC

Amen	*The Contemporary Hymn Book* David Yantis Publications
The Apostle's Creed Father Clarence Jos. Rivers	Sheet music Stimuli, Inc.
Ave Verum Corpus Mozart	Sheet music Pro-Art Publications, Inc.
But Then Comes the Morning	*Young People's Folk Hymnal*, Vol. II World Library of Sacred Music
Climb Every Mountain	*The Sound of Music* Williamson Music, Inc.
Come before the Table of the Lord	*Young People's Folk Hymnal*, Vol. I World Library of Sacred Music
Consolation	*Songs of All Time* Cooperative Recreation Serv., Inc.
Dakota Hymn	*Songs of Many Nations* World Around Songs Publication
Day Is Done	*Maranatha Song Book* (lyrics and guitar chords only) Maranatha Publications Sheet music Warner Bros. Seven Arts Music
From the Voices of Children	*Young People's Folk Hymnal*, Vol. II World Library of Sacred Music
Glory	*Young People's Folk Hymnal*, Vol. II World Library of Sacred Music

God Gives His People Strength The Medical Mission Sisters	*Joy Is Like the Rain* Song Book Vanguard Music Corp.
God Made the World	*Young People's Folk Hymnal*, Vol. II World Library of Sacred Music
God the Father Father Clarence Jos. Rivers	Sheet music Stimuli, Inc.
Go Tell It on the Mountain	*The Contemporary Hymn Book* David Yantis Publications *Peter, Paul and Mary Song Book* Warner Bros. Seven Arts Music
Hava Nageela Roger Wagner Chorale	Sheet music G. Schirmer, Inc.
He Ain't Heavy, He's My Brother	*Maranatha Song Book* Maranatha Publications Sheet music Shawnee Press
Here Comes Jesus	*Electric Church Song Book* Sacred Songs *Maranatha Song Book* Maranatha Publications
He's Got the Whole World in His Hands	*Maranatha Song Book* Maranatha Publications *The Contemporary Hymn Book* David Yantis Publications

Hymn
  Paul Stookey

Sheet music
  Warner Bros. Seven Arts Music
Maranatha Song Book
  Maranatha Publications

I Built a Garden
The Medical
Mission Sisters

Sheet music
  Vanguard Music Corp.

I Don't Know How
to Love Him
(Mary's Song)

Jesus Christ, Superstar
  Leeds Music Ltd.

Joshua Fit De
Battle of Jericho

American Negro Spirituals
  James Weldon and
    J. Rosamond Johnson
  Viking Press

Joy Is Like the Rain

Joy Is Like the Rain Song Book
  Vanguard Music Corp.

The Joy Song

The Contemporary Hymn Book
  David Yantis Publications
Joan Baez Song Book
  Ryerson Music Pub.

Kum-By-Ya

The Contemporary Hymn Book
  David Yantis Publications
Joan Baez Song Book
  Ryerson Music Pub.

Let's Get Together
  Hal Leonard

New Wine Song Book
  So. Calif. Conf. Methodist Church

Let Us Break Bread
Together

The Contemporary Hymn Book
  David Yantis Publications

The Man

He's Everything to Me Song Book
  Lexicon Music, Inc.

The Man for Me

The Ylvisaker Hymnerie
  Vanguard Music Corp.

My Sweet Lord
  George Harrison

Sheet music
  Chas. Hansen Publishers

No Man Is An
Island
  Joan Whitney &
  Alex Kramer

Sheet music
  Bourne Company,

O Happy Day
  Edward R.
  Hawkins

Sheet music
  United Artists Music Co., Inc.

Oh, Sing to the
Lord a New Song
  Fred Prentiss

Sheet music
  Sacred Songs

Pass It On
  Ralph Carmichael
  & Kurt Kaiser

Tell It Like It Is
  Sacred Songs

Peace, My Friends

F.E.L. Song Book, Vol. IV
  F.E.L. Publications

Praise Christ, the
Son of the Living
God
  Father Clarence
  Jos. Rivers

Sheet music
  Stimuli, Inc.

Put Your Hand
in the Hand

Maranatha Song Book
  Maranatha Publications
Sheet music
  Studio Press

Ride On, King Jesus
  Father Clarence
  Jos. Rivers

Book: *Celebration*
  Herder and Herder

Robert Shaw Chorale	Sheet music Lawson Gould Music Pub., Inc.	This Land Is Your Land	New Wine Song Book So. Calif. Conf. Methodist Church
Rock-a-My-Soul	Maranatha Song Book Maranatha Publications Peter, Paul and Mary Song Book Warner Bros. Seven Arts Music	Try a Little Kindness	Maranatha Song Book Maranatha Publications Sheet music Charles Hansen Pub.
Seek and Ye Shall Find	Maranatha Song Book Maranatha Publications The Contemporary Hymn Book David Yantis Publications	Twenty-third Psalm (Retitled "Resignation")	Songs of All Time Cooperative Recreation Serv., Inc.
Shalom	Sheet music G. Schirmer, Inc.	You've Got a Friend	Maranatha Song Book Maranatha Publications Screen Gems, Columbia Music, Inc.
The Spirit Is a-Movin'	Listen—Agape Singers, Vol. II Louisville Area Council of Churches	We're Called to Be That City	Some Young Carpenter World Library of Sacred Music
Sweet Sweet Song of Salvation Larry Norman	Sheet music Beechwood Music Co.	Were You There	The Contemporary Hymn Book David Yantis Publications American Negro Spirituals Viking Press Maranatha Song Book Maranatha Publications
Swing Low, Sweet Chariot	The Contemporary Hymn Book David Yantis Publications American Negro Spirituals Viking Press	The Wedding Banquet	Joy Is Like the Rain Song Book Vanguard Music Corp.
Thank You, Jesus	Sheet music Sacred Songs	When the Saints Go Marching In	The Contemporary Hymn Book David Yantis Publications
They'll Know We Are Christians by Our Love	Hymnal for Young Christians F.E.L. Publications Ltd. Sacred Songs, Vol. II Sacred Songs	Where Do I See God	The Contemporary Hymn Book David Yantis Publications

MUSIC PUBLISHERS

Beechwood Music Co.
1750 Vine Street
Hollywood, Calif. 90028

Bourne Company
136 West 52nd Street
New York, N. Y. 10019

Charles Hansen
1842 West Ave.
Miami Beach, Fla. 33139

Cooperative Recreation Serv. Inc.
511 State Route 203
Delaware, Ohio

David Yantis Publications
1505 - 47th St.
San Diego, Calif. 92102

F.E.L. Publications, Ltd.
1543 West Olympic Blvd.
Los Angeles, Calif. 90015

F.E.L. Publications, Ltd.
1307 S. Wabash Ave.
Chicago, Ill. 60605

Gospel Quartet Music Co.
1750 North Vine St.
Hollywood, Calif, 90028

G. Schirmer, Inc.
609 Fifth Ave.
New York, N. Y.

Hal Leonard Publications
64 East Second St.
Winona, Minn.

Herder and Herder
232 Madison Ave.
New York, N. Y. 10022

Lawson Gould Music Publishers, Inc.
609 Fifth Ave.
New York, N. Y.

Leeds Music, Ltd.
445 Park Ave.
New York, N. Y.

Lexicon Music, Inc.
Box 296
Woodland Hills, Calif.

Louisville Area Council of Churches
210 Y.M.C.A. Building
Louisville, Ky.

Maranatha Publications
P. O. Box 672
Saratoga, Calif. 95070

Ryerson Music Publisher
154 West 14th St.
New York, N. Y. 10011

Sacred Songs
Box 1790
Waco, Texas 76703

Screen Gems, Columbia Music, Inc.
7033 W. Sunset Blvd.
Los Angeles, Calif 90028

Shawnee Press
Delaware Water Gap,
Penna. 18327

So. Calif. Conference Methodist Ch.
5250 Santa Monica Blvd.
Los Angeles, Calif. 90029

Stimuli, Inc.
17 Erkenbrecker
Cincinnati, Ohio 45220

Studio Press
224 S. Lebanon St.
Lebanon, Indiana 46052

United Artists Music Co., Inc.
729 Seventh Ave.
New York, N. Y. 10019

Vanguard Music Corp.
520 West 57th St.
New York, N. Y. 10019

Viking Press
625 Madison Ave.
New York, N. Y. 10022

Warner Bros. Seven Arts Music
488 Madison Ave.
New York, N. Y. 10022

Williamson Music, Inc.
609 Fifth Ave.
New York, N. Y. 10017

World Around Songs Publications
Informal Music Service
United Church of Christ

World Library of Sacred Music
2145 Central Parkway
Cincinnati, Ohio

Backwards | *Uncovered Feelings*
By Herbert F. Brokering
Fortress Press

Benediction | *Uncovered Feelings*
By Herbert F. Brokering
Fortress Press

The Creation | *God's Trombones*
By James Weldon Johnson
The Viking Press

Creed | *Uncovered Feelings*
By Herbert F. Brokering
Fortress Press

Eight | *Listen to the Warm*
By Rod McKuen
Random House, Inc.

For the Sin of Terricide | *New Prayers For The High Holy Days*
Selection by Paul Flucke
Ed. Rabbi Jack Riemer
Prayer Book Press

The Giving Tree | *The Giving Tree*
By Shel Silverstein
Harper and Row

Holy Communion | *Footnotes and Headlines*
By Corita Kent
Herder and Herder

I know it sounds corny, Jesus, but I'm lonely | *Are You Running With Me, Jesus?*
By Malcolm Boyd
Holt, Rinehart & Winston

Involvement | *Innocent No More*
By Marilee Zdenek

It's a Groovy Day, Lord! | A Prayer
By Rabbi Allen Secher

I've searched for community in many places, Jesus | *Are You Running With Me, Jesus?*
By Malcolm Boyd
Holt, Rinehart & Winston

The Kingdom of Heaven Is Like An Open Hydrant on a Hot Summer Day | *Full Circle*
By Kevin McNiff
Full Circle Associates

Renewal | *Innocent No More*
By Marilee Zdenek

Tied | *Uncovered Feelings*
By Herbert F. Brokering
Fortress Press

What If God Danced Instead of Walked? | *Words Are No Good If the Game Is Solitaire*
By Herbert B. Barks
Word Books

The Wire Fence | *Prayers*
By Michel Quoist
Sheed and Ward

You Are like the Noonday Sun in the Night | *I Lie On My Mat and Pray*
Prayers by Young Africans
Friendship Press

FILMS	FILM COMPANIES	POSTER COMPANIES
		Abbey Press
Autumn: Frost Country	Pyramid Films	St. Meinrad, Indiana
	Box 1048	
	Santa Monica, Calif. 90406	Argus Communications
Creatures, Bless the Lord	Franciscan Communications	3505 North Ashland Ave.
	Center	Chicago, Ill. 60657
	1229 South Santee St.	
	Los Angeles, Calif. 90015	Full Circle Associates
His Land	World Wide Pictures	218 East 72nd Street
	1313 Hennepin Ave.	New York, N. Y. 10021
	Minneapolis, Minn. 55403	
The Kiss	Franciscan Communications	Geo. A. Pflaum, Publisher, Inc.
	Center	38 West Fifth St.
Listen, Lady	Franciscan Communications	Dayton, Ohio 45402
	Center	
Person to Person	Franciscan Communications	
	Center	FELT & STITCHERY BANNERS
Pollution	Argus Communications	AND BANNER PATTERNS
	3505 North Ashland Ave.	
	Chicago, Ill. 60657	Jean Pegram
Psalm for a Surfer	Franciscan Communications	1126 Stradella Road
	Center	Los Angeles, Calif. 90024
Restricted Neighborhood	Franciscan Communications	
	Center	PAINTED VINYL BANNERS
Say 'Yes' to Love	Franciscan Communications	
	Center	Gloria Wood
		1417 Havenhurst
		Los Angeles, Calif. 90046

Catalogs are available from some of these companies.

Graphics......... Ron Riddick
Photos......... Don Heath
                Helen Drysdale
Drawings....... Lad Odell
                Ron Riddick
Banners...... Jean Pegram
              Gloria Wood
              and
              Beverly Hills Pres.

ACKNOWLEDGMENTS

Grateful acknowledgment is made to the owners and copyright holders listed below for their permission to quote from previously published material:

Fortress Press, for the poems "Benediction," "Backwards," "Creed," and "Tied" from *Uncovered Feelings* by Herbert Brokering.

Friendship Press, for the poem "You Are Like the Noonday Sun in the Night" from *I Lie on My Mat and Pray, Prayers by Young Africans*, edited by Fritz Pawelzik, published by Friendship Press, 1964. Used by permission.

Full Circle Associates, for "The Kingdom of Heaven Is Like an Open Hydrant on a Hot Summer Day" by Kevin McNiff.

Herder and Herder, for "Holy Communion" from *Footnotes and Headlines* by Corita Kent.

Holt, Rinehart and Winston, Inc., for the prayers "I know it sounds corny, Jesus, but I'm lonely" and "I've searched for community in many places, Jesus" from *Are You Running with Me, Jesus?* by Malcolm Boyd. Copyright © 1965 by Malcolm Boyd. Reprinted by permission of Holt, Rinehart and Winston, Inc.

Rod McKuen Enterprises, for the poem "Eight" from *Listen to the Warm*, copyright © 1967 by Warm Music. Used by permission of the author.

Prayer Book Press, for "The Sin of Terricide" by Paul Flucke from *New Prayers for the High Holy Days*, ed. Rabbi Jack Riemer, copyright 1970, Prayer Book Press, Bridgeport, Connecticut.

Rabbi Allen Secher, for his prayer "It Was a Groovy Day, Lord."

Sheed & Ward Inc., for "The Wire Fence" from *Prayers* by Michel Quoist, © Sheed & Ward Inc., 1963.

Word, Inc., for "If God doesn't fizz, how come I feel all these bubbles?" and "What If God Danced Instead of Walked?" from *Words Are No Good If the Game Is Solitaire* by Herbert B. Barks, Jr., copyright © 1971 by Word, Inc.

Beechwood Music Corporation, for a portion of the lyrics of "Try a Little Kindness," © 1969 Airefield Music, A Division of Beechwood Music Corporation/Glen Campbell Music, words and music by Bobby Austin and Curt Sapaugh; and for the lyrics of "Sweet Sweet Song of Salvation," © 1970 Beechwood Music Corporation/J. C. Love Publishing Company, words and music by Larry Norman.

F.E.L. Publications, Ltd., for lyrics from "They'll Know We Are Christians" by Peter Scholtes, copyright © 1966, F.E.L. Publications, Ltd., 1543 W. Olympic Blvd., Los Angeles, Calif. 90015. Used with permission.

Irving Music, Inc., for lyrics from "Let's Get Together" by Chet Powers, © 1963 Irving Music Inc. (B.M.I.). All rights reserved.

Stimuli Inc., for lyrics from the responses "God the Father, hear our prayer" and "Praise Christ the Son of the Living God" by Father Clarence Jos. Rivers, © Stimuli Inc., Box 20066, Cincinnati, Ohio 45220.

Vanguard Music Corp., for the words from "The Wedding Banquet" by Sister Miriam Therese Winter, © MCMLXV by Medical Mission Sisters. Sole selling agent Vanguard Music Corp., 250 W. 57th St., N.Y., N.Y. 10019. Permission granted to reprint by Vanguard Music Corp. "The Wedding Banquet" is available on album #AVS 101 from Avant Garde Records, Inc., 250 W. 57th St., N.Y., N.Y. 10019.

Warner Bros. Music, for lyrics from "Day Is Done" by Peter Yarrow, copyright © 1969 by Pepamar Music Corp. All rights reserved. Used by permission of Warner Bros. Music.

World Library Publications, Inc., for lyrics from "Forgive, Lord, Forgive," "From the Voices of Children," "God Made the World," "There Are But Three Things That Last," and "We're Called to Be That City."

Scripture quotations from *The New Testament in Modern English*, translated by J. B. Phillips, © J. B. Phillips 1958. Published by The Macmillan Company, and used by their permission.

Scripture quotations from The Revised Standard Version of the Bible, copyright © 1946 and 1952 by the Division of Christian Education of the National Council of the Churches of Christ in the USA are used by permission.

Scripture quotations from The Today's English Version of the Bible, Good News for Modern Man, copyright © American Bible Society 1966. Used by permission.

Photographs on pp. 141, 142, 143, 153 are by Mary Ann Gehres, *Presbyterian Life*.

Photographs on pp. 98, 99, 100, 101, 114, 115, 122 are by Helen Drysdale.

Photographs on pp. 46, 48, 49, 50, 52, 62, 64, 65, 76, 77, 112, 123, 124 are by Don Heath.